SPOOKY
New York

Tales of Hauntings, Strange Happenings, and Other Local Lore

RETOLD BY S. E. SCHLOSSER

ILLUSTRATED BY PAUL G. HOFFMAN

INSIDERS' GUIDE®

GUILFORD, CONNECTICUT
AN IMPRINT OF THE GLOBE PEQUOT PRESS

For my "aunt" Sandy Thomas, and for my third "sister" Barbara Strobel. Thanks for the all the good times and the great advice.

For my family—David, Dena, Tim, Arlene, Hannah, Emma, Nathan, Benjamin, Deb, Gabe, Clare, Jack, and Karen.

For the New Media gang—Jerry, Tony, Len, Paula, Sue, and Anne— who have patiently listened to me talk about all things spooky from Maine to Texas and back again.

For Richard and for the Bryce family. And in memory of Mark Bryce.

In memory of my grandparents Harold and Lola Dawson, and of my aunt and uncle Gilbert and Ellen Dawson.

***

To buy books in quantity for corporate use
or incentives, call **(800) 962–0973**
or e-mail **premiums@GlobePequot.com.**

INSIDERS' GUIDE®

Text design by Lisa Reneson
Illustrations and map border by Paul G. Hoffman
Map by Stefanie Ward © Morris Book Publishing, LLC

Library of Congress Cataloging-in-Publication Data is available.

ISBN 978-0-7627-3426-9

Manufactured in the United States of America
First Edition/Third Printing

Contents

Contents

Contents

SPOOKY SITES . . .

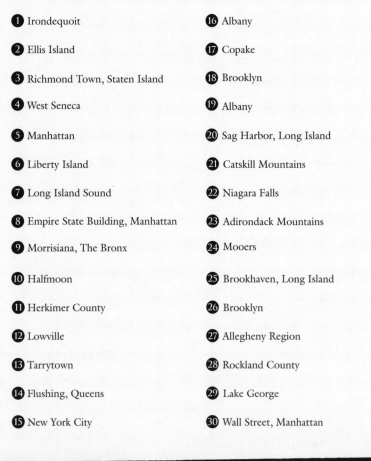

1. Irondequoit
2. Ellis Island
3. Richmond Town, Staten Island
4. West Seneca
5. Manhattan
6. Liberty Island
7. Long Island Sound
8. Empire State Building, Manhattan
9. Morrisiana, The Bronx
10. Halfmoon
11. Herkimer County
12. Lowville
13. Tarrytown
14. Flushing, Queens
15. New York City
16. Albany
17. Copake
18. Brooklyn
19. Albany
20. Sag Harbor, Long Island
21. Catskill Mountains
22. Niagara Falls
23. Adirondack Mountains
24. Mooers
25. Brookhaven, Long Island
26. Brooklyn
27. Allegheny Region
28. Rockland County
29. Lake George
30. Wall Street, Manhattan

AND WHERE TO FIND THEM

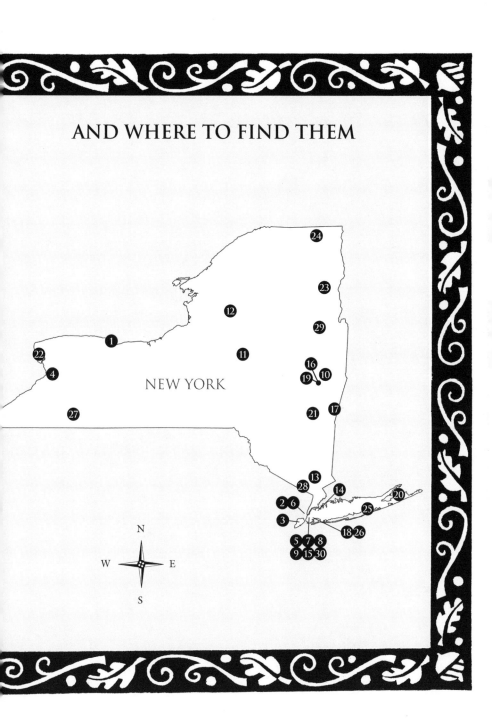

Contents

Introduction

I love New York. I know that sounds trite, but it's the truth. This is the land of Washington Irving, the land of the Baker's Dozen, the place where spending the night in a hermit's cabin can be very bad for your health, and the place where a willow tree withered because Benedict Arnold touched it after he betrayed his country to the British. Ghosts ice-skate in Central Park, werewolves roam the north woods, gnomes play ninepins in the Catskill Mountains, and a Hessian gallops through Sleepy Hollow. There is a plethora of folklore in this wonderful state, and this collection is just the tip of the iceberg. I wish I had room to relate all the tales I know about New York!

I grew up in the shadow of New York City, and this, perhaps, explains my fascination with New York folktales, especially those of the spooky sort. As a small child, I remember taking class trips to famous spots in New York City. My legs still feel sore when I recall the climb to the crown of Lady Liberty—an exciting adventure, or so I thought at the time. Looking back now, I am disappointed that my teacher did not mention that Captain Kidd had buried his treasure on that self-same Liberty Island. I am certain that my father would have let me borrow a shovel to take with me on our class trip, and I could probably have dug up all the treasure and still made it back to the ferry in time.

Another teacher on another trip took my class to the observation deck of the Empire State Building. Little did I know that I should have been watching for a ghost instead of gaping at the view. I blame the education system. My teachers kept insisting that I learn the multiplication tables instead of reading spooky folktales. Just think of all the opportunities I have missed due to a lack of spooky information!

In summer, I would attend sleep-away camp in the Adirondacks, where I learned to make lanyards, paddle a canoe, and scare the dickens out of younger campers by telling them the creepiest ghost stories I could make up. After a few nights of this, even my counselor went a little green when she had to walk down a certain spooky path after dark. Of course, she got back at me by relating some of the scary folktales that have floated around the Adirondacks since the very first settlers moved into the mountains. After that, I was the one who turned green at the thought of sleeping in the dark.

My love affair with New York continued when I attended college in the Western Tier, earning my Bachelor of Music Education from Houghton College, which is just an hour southeast of Buffalo. It was during my college years that I encountered the tale of the Maid of the Mist when visiting Niagara Falls, and, of course, I heard many spooky stories about ghosts, ghoulies, and other dark creatures that haunt the Western Tier. Coincidentally, one of my favorite ghosts (Redemption) used to be a resident of West Seneca, the town in which I lived while I was doing my student teaching.

Later, I would spend time in the Catskills, where I attended music festivals and kept a lookout for Henry Hudson and his crew, since I thought it would be splendid fun to play a game of ninepins with them (but don't drink the wine, folks, unless you want to sleep for twenty years).

After moving around a bit, I finally made my home in New York State. Every weekday, I drive through the Ramapo mountains (I must confess that I have never encountered the Ramapo Salamander); cross the Hudson River at Tappan Zee; pass the Tarrytown and Sleepy Hollow exit on the thruway (no sign of the Galloping Hessian); and make my way down to Yonkers. Honestly, if I could have just one ghostly encounter, the IRS might consider my daily commute tax deductible.

I would have welcomed a view of the Ghost Ship of the Hudson (which warns people of the coming of storms) on the afternoon I drove right into a giant thunderstorm as it was sweeping its way across the Hudson River. If I had seen the ghost ship, I might have pulled off the road before I got to the Tappan Zee, rather than sweating out the storm on a windswept, rain-lashed, slippery bridge. That was the only time I was ever happy to be surrounded by tractor trailers, since they bore the brunt of the wind.

If none of the above statements are enough to explain my infatuation with New York, surely the fact that eight generations of my family have resided in the state is all the reason I need. My many-times great-grandfather was a captain of a ship that worked the Erie Canal. My twice great-grandfather and his son farmed the land south of Syracuse. My grandmother went to school in Horseheads (I refuse to tell you how *that* town got its name!) before marrying my grandfather, who lived in Cortland and worked for Western Union. His brother, my great-uncle Gib, spent World War II interpreting top-secret intelligence telegraphs for the White House and later was part of the press core surrounding FDR before settling once more in Cortland, where he and his wife helped my widowed grandmother raise my mother. To cap it all off, my parents met in New York, sweethearting in Syracuse while my father was attending law school.

So, really, is it any wonder that I love New York? My roots are buried deep in this land, and I may claim a piece of its rich, spooky heritage, because it is my own.

—Sandy Schlosser

PART ONE
Ghost Stories

1

The White Lady of the Lake

IRONDEQUOIT

I must have tried on ten outfits before I finally decided what I was going to wear on my very first date with Jeff. I had been on the phone all afternoon with one friend after the other, discussing colors, accessories, nail polish, and all the other style essentials that I normally don't think about, since I consider myself an intellectual rather than a fashion plate. But that was before I was asked out by the most popular boy in school.

I went out on the front porch to polish my toenails. I was a third of the way through when a familiar shadow blocked the warm spring sunshine for a moment. I didn't even look up.

"What is it now, Stan?" I asked wearily. My neighbor since birth shuffled his way into the wicker chair next to mine.

"Listen, Jamie, is it true Jeff is taking you on a picnic to Durand-Eastman Park?"

Good grief, I thought. Jeff had just made the final arrangements with me half an hour ago. I had, of course, immediately phoned my best friend, Diane, and told her the news. Assuming it took Diane at least ten minutes to call all our other friends, and then another ten minutes for them to call their friends, that would mean that the news must have reached Stan within twenty-five minutes after I hung up with Jeff. That had to be some kind of gossiping record, I concluded, looking over at Stan.

Stan looks a bit like a sandy-haired scarecrow. He's 6 feet 2 inches and naturally plays basketball, but outside the court he appears a bit awkward, as if he has two left feet. Stan is also an intellectual, like me. I consider him a good friend, except for his irritating habit of asking me to go out with him at least once a month. I mean, I like Stan, but just as a friend.

"We are going to the park," I answered his question. "Why?"

"I think you should ask Jeff to take you to the movies," said Stan. "The park is a bad idea."

"What do you mean, a bad idea?" I asked suspiciously. Now what was Stan up to? Was he trying to break my date with Jeff?

"Come on, Jamie, even you must have heard about the White Lady," Stan said.

I stared at Stan incredulously for a moment, and then started to laugh. "For a second there, I thought you were serious," I gasped. "The White Lady! For goodness sake, Stan, no one believes that old story!"

Stan frowned and I stopped laughing. He couldn't be serious! But apparently he was.

The White Lady was the most famous ghost around Rochester (she haunts the Rochester suburb Irondequoit, just to the north). In the early 1800s, the White Lady and her daughter were supposed to have lived on the land where

Durand-Eastman Park now stands. Then one day, the daughter disappeared. Convinced that the girl had been harmed and killed by a local farmer, the mother, accompanied by her two German shepherds, searched the marshy lands day after day for her child's body. She never found a trace of her daughter and finally, in her grief, committed suicide. Her faithful dogs pined for their mistress after her death, and soon followed her to the grave. The mother's spirit returned to continue the search for her child. People say that on foggy nights, the White Lady and her dogs rise from Durand Lake. Together, they roam through the park, looking for the missing daughter and seeking vengeance against men. Any man who catches the ghost's eye had best beware, for the White Lady and her dogs are killers. Or at least that's the version of the story I heard at school.

"Come on, Stan. You don't really believe there is a White Lady," I said. "I mean, ghosts? Please!"

"I would still feel much better about the whole thing if you and Jeff went to the movies," Stan said stubbornly.

"I'm touched by your concern," I said sarcastically. "But I am sure we will be just fine. Now, I have to go change. Jeff is picking me up at 6:30."

I left Stan sitting morosely on my porch and went to prepare for my date.

Jeff pulled into my driveway promptly at 6:30 P.M. in his yellow convertible. He was polite and polished with my parents, assuring them he would have me home by curfew, and then he tucked me into the front seat next to him. I could smell fried chicken coming from the picnic basket.

Stan was sitting in a rocker on his porch, watching us as we drove off. Jeff nodded stiffly to him; Stan nodded back.

"I didn't know you lived next door to Stan," Jeff said.

"All my life," I said. Just then my cell phone rang. I answered it, and Stan said, "Tell Jeff that you want to go to the movies."

"Give me a break, Stan," I said, and hung up.

Jeff glanced over at me. "What did Stan want?" he asked.

"Stan thinks we should go to the movies instead of to the park," I explained. "He thinks the White Lady will come and get us if we go there."

Jeff laughed. "I didn't think Stan was so superstitious!" he said. "Or is he jealous?" he asked, glancing at me again.

"I don't know!" I said impishly. "Maybe!"

We laughed and talked all the way to the park. Jeff parked the car in the lot next to Lake Ontario, and we crossed the street to what he called "the White Lady's castle," which overlooks both Lake Ontario and the smaller Lake Durand, a lovely, tree-shrouded lake directly across the street from Lake Ontario. We climbed up the stairs and spread the blanket out on the grassy spot at the top, behind the cobblestone wall. I unpacked the picnic basket, and we sat munching fried chicken and comparing notes about our teachers. Then Jeff started making some sly, rather uncomplimentary remarks about Stan, which I didn't appreciate. I guess he didn't like Stan calling me and telling me not to go to the park. When I didn't respond to his witticism, Jeff changed the subject, embarking upon a monologue of his athletic exploits, which, frankly, bored me to tears. Jeff was really cute, but I prefer my guys to have a bit more modesty than Jeff was currently displaying.

It was dusk when I heard a crashing noise and a familiar muffled cursing coming from the trees behind us. I knew at once that it was Stan. Jeff looked around.

"What was that?" he asked lazily.

"Just some kids fooling around," I said, glaring at Stan, who retreated behind a tree. *Go home*, I mouthed at him and turned to smile at Jeff.

"Fooling around, eh?" Jeff said, giving me a wicked grin. "Sounds like fun!"

Jeff leaned toward me, and I jumped up and walked over to the right side of the wall to look out at Durand Lake. I wasn't going to kiss that vain bore, even to get back at Stan.

To my right, the mist was rising off Durand Lake and the light was growing dim. I could see Stan scrambling down the hill toward the lake as silently as he could. He looked upset, but it served him right for following me on my date. Then I heard a step behind me and Jeff slid his arms around my waist.

"What's the matter, Jamie? Are you playing hard to get?" he asked, nuzzling my neck.

I was watching the mist over the lake, which was swirling strangely. I blinked a few times and suddenly realized that I was seeing a beautiful woman solidifying before my eyes. Two smaller swirls beside her became German shepherds. The White Lady was watching Stan, who had just reached the road at the bottom of the hill. She did not look happy to see him. Stan did not look happy to see her either. For a moment, my neighbor and the ghost stared at one another. The dogs at her side bristled, baring their teeth at him. Then the ghost gestured to the dogs and they ran toward Stan. Stan hightailed it

THE WHITE LADY OF THE LAKE

back up the slope as fast as he could go, the ghost dogs snapping at his heels. The White Lady's face transformed from that of a beautiful woman to that of a haggard witch. She started rising up from the surface of the lake, following the crashing sounds Stan was making as he ran up the hill.

"Don't be so shy," Jeff said, nuzzling my hair.

Just then, the White Lady caught a glimpse of me and Jeff cuddled up next to the wall. Stan was forgotten in an instant. I stiffened as the ghost, accompanied by her two dogs, started rushing toward us! Feeling me tense, Jeff looked up and saw the White Lady for the first time. He let go of me so fast that I fell against the wall. Jeff didn't even notice. He was too busy stumbling backward, gasping swear words, and falling over the picnic basket. I was frozen to the spot, praying that the stories about the White Lady were true, and that she protected females rather than killing them. The White Lady ignored me completely. I ducked as she sailed right over my head in a rush of freezing cold air. She was aiming for Jeff with a look of murder on her face, and Jeff didn't wait around. He flew around the wall and half-ran half-stumbled down the stairs, the White Lady on his heels.

I grabbed my cell phone and ran to the top of the steps just as two enormous, semitransparent German shepherds flew across the wall in pursuit of their mistress. I jumped out of their way and watched Jeff running across the road and down the hill towards Lake Ontario, the White Lady and her dogs in hot pursuit. I flipped open my cell phone, started to dial 9-1-1, then paused. The emergency staff would think I was a kook if I reported a malicious ectoplasm chasing my date into the lake.

Who *do* you call when a ghost gets out of hand?

Jeff plunged into the lake and submerged. The White Lady floated over the place he disappeared, looking very upset and very determined.

Just then, I heard someone call my name. I turned around. Stan was at the edge of the woods, looking nervously at the ghosts hovering over the water. I was relieved to see him in one piece.

"Are you okay?" he called.

I nodded and waved him into the woods, afraid of what the White Lady might do if she saw him. Then I turned back to see what was happening to Jeff.

The White Lady was floating back and forth over the water discontentedly. There was no sign of Jeff. *He has to be making some kind of world record for holding his breath,* I mused. The White Lady turned slowly toward shore and started floating up, up, up to the overlook until she drew even with me. The ghost and I looked at each other for a moment. Finally, she nodded to me, her face once again beautiful. Then she beckoned to the dogs, and together they floated out over Durand Lake, growing dimmer and dimmer until they had faded away completely.

I turned back toward Lake Ontario and saw Jeff's head come bursting out of the water. He gasped desperately for air, looking around for the White Lady.

"Jeff!" I shouted. "She's gone!"

I started running down the stairs as Jeff raced from the lake. He looked neither right nor left. He just ran straight up the bank and into the parking lot, leaped into his car, and roared away. I stopped halfway down the steps, my mouth hanging open. *He left me,* I thought blankly. *That no-good rotter left me alone with the ghost and her two dogs.*

It was almost completely dark now. I walked slowly back up the stairs, wondering what to do. Mechanically, I gathered up the remains of the picnic and folded up the blanket. Then I flipped open my cell phone and dialed a familiar number.

"Yes?" Stan answered on the first ring.

"Did you see that?" I demanded into my phone.

"I saw that," Stan said, keeping his voice neutral.

"He left me! He didn't even try to find out if I was all right," I said indignantly. "Would you give me a ride home?"

"I'd be happy to," said Stan. He hesitated a moment and then said, "You know, there's still time to catch a late movie."

I thought about it. On the one hand, there was handsome, popular Jeff who had left me to the mercy of the White Lady. On the other hand, there was my faithful Stan, who had been chased by the White Lady's dogs and had come back to make sure I was all right. Of course, this whole scene might have been an elaborate plot by Stan to get a date with me. Still, the ghosts had *seemed* real.

"Okay," I said into the phone.

There was a stunned pause, and then Stan said, "I'll bring the car to the bottom of the stairs." He hung up.

I could hear his whoop of utter happiness all the way across the park. A moment later, I heard a car engine start, and I knew he was on his way to pick me up. I grabbed the picnic basket and started down the stairs, grinning from ear to ear, to meet Stan.

2

The Party at Wild Goose Tavern

ELLIS ISLAND

Way back before the great immigrant station dominated its shores, Ellis Island was known as Gibbet Island because it was the favored spot for hanging pirates, mutineers, and other evil-doers. The British authorities intended to discourage lawless behavior with such dramatic displays, and for a time it worked. The good Dutch folk living in Communipaw, on the western side of the Hudson, were dissuaded from openly behaving in a less-than-moral way, and the community prospered.

The sole exception was a rogue named Yan Yost Vanderscamp, who seemed destined to rebel against authority whenever possible. Vanderscamp was the nephew of the land-lord of the Wild Goose Tavern, and true to his name, he was as mischievous and twisted a scamp as ever set foot in Communipaw. The sleepy Dutch burghers who gathered together to smoke and drink Hollands during the long winter evenings viewed the lad with alarm whenever he set foot in the bar, having experienced his practical jokes more than once. No one was surprised when Vanderscamp became a pirate as soon as he was old enough to leave home.

Yan took his friend Pluto to sea with him, and soon they had gathered together a boisterous band of pirates, who preyed upon honest folk up and down the shores of the Atlantic. Periodically, Yan would come home to Communipaw to visit the Wild Goose Tavern and plague the honest, God-fearing folks in the community.

When his uncle died, Vanderscamp inherited the Wild Goose Tavern. Such was the drinking, gaming, swearing, and general uproar caused by Vanderscamp's men when they took over the tavern that the good Dutch burghers abandoned the Wild Goose completely. The people of Communipaw petitioned the British authorities to help them end the disgraceful goings-on in their quiet community. In response, the authorities laid a trap for the swashbuckling buccaneers late one night. They managed to catch three of the pirates before the others escaped. The British strung Vanderscamp's men up on Gibbet Island and left their bodies hanging there in chains as a warning to their fellow pirates. The boisterous behavior stopped after that night, though the Dutch burghers still did not feel comfortable enough to visit the tavern. Vanderscamp and his men came and went in secret, and mysterious lights would appear late at night when good folk should be in bed and asleep.

About a month following the British raid on the Wild Goose Tavern, Vanderscamp and Pluto paid a late night visit to their pirate ship. As they were sailing back to Communipaw, a squall broke, forcing them to shelter in the lee of Gibbet Island, where their comrades had been executed. The lightning flashed, the rain beat down, and the thunder roared over-

THE PARTY AT WILD GOOSE TAVERN

head as Yan Yost Vanderscamp and Pluto huddled miserably aboard their skiff, the bodies of their hung companions swaying above them in the brutal wind, rags fluttering and chains grinding.

Yan shrank away from the grisly sight, drinking deeply from his bottle of rum. Pluto jeered at him, scorn filling his eyes and creasing his face. He said, "You claim that you fear no man, living or dead. Why do you shrink away from your friends?"

"I do not fear them," Yan said sharply. He took another swig from his bottle and then raised it toward the bodies of his dead companions and cried, "Here's to you lads! If you should care to go walking tonight, make sure you visit the Wild Goose Tavern for supper!"

The wind roared about the corpses, rattling the chains and creaking the bones of the dead pirates. For a moment, it sounded as if the dead men were laughing in response to Yan's words. Vanderscamp sat down quickly. "Let us leave here," he said to Pluto. His friend nodded, speechless for once.

It was midnight before they reached Communipaw, and the storm continued to lash at them as Vanderscamp and Pluto ran to the Wild Goose Tavern. As Yan entered the building, the sound of boisterous singing and the clanking of bottles reached his ears. Yan was furious. A party was being held upstairs in his absence!

Yan took the stairs two at a time and threw open the door. Seated at the table inside the room were three twisted, withered corpses. Yan gasped as he recognized the dead comrades he had toasted on Gibbet Island. The table was set for a meal, and each corpse held a tankard of ale. The candles lighting the room were burning with a strange blue color that seemed to highlight the ropes around the necks of the dead pirates and the chains binding hands and feet. They were clinking their tankards together and singing their favorite drinking song. When they saw Yan, the corpses gave a roar of greeting and beckoned for him to join them at their grisly feast.

Yan gave a shout of pure terror and threw himself backward, away from the sinister scene. His foot slipped on the top step, and he plunged down the stairs, landing with a terrible clatter, his head hitting the floor with a very final-sounding *thump.*

The neighbors found him at the foot of the stairs the next morning and had him buried in the churchyard for the sake of his sainted uncle. The tavern had been deserted by the buccaneers, and all the ill-gotten plunder was gone. At first, the people of Communipaw assumed that Pluto had killed Yan and escaped with the loot. Then Pluto's drowned body was found on the following day, lodged among the rocks just below the swaying bodies of his fellow pirates. So Yan's death remained an unsolved mystery.

For many years afterward, no honest person would set foot upon Gibbet Island. Several times, holy folk tried to purge the island with bell, book, and candle, for it was said to be haunted by dark shadows and strange lights. But their efforts never completely rid the island of its ghosts. To this day, boatmen passing the island at night will sometimes hear the creak and groan of chains swaying in the wind as they near the site of the pirates' execution, and some have even caught glimpses of Vanderscamp and his pirates wandering its shores.

3

The Gray Lady

RICHMOND TOWN, STATEN ISLAND

My grandkids find it hard to believe that their all-American, Yankee grandfather actually fought for the wrong side in the Revolutionary War. But it's true. I came to America as part of the British Army sent to quell the uprising in the Colonies. It wasn't until after the war that I decided this was the place for me and settled permanently in the newly formed United States of America, taking me a Yankee bride.

I was with a Scottish regiment and we were stationed in Richmond Town. There were a number of Tories on the island, and their pretty daughters flirted and danced with the officers, which caused a ruckus at times. There were at least two men—boyhood chums of mine serving in the same Highland regiment—who got themselves in a bad way over a Tory girl. To this day their fate angers me.

She was a pretty girl with fair hair, large blue eyes, and pink cheeks. The men all called her "Rosie," though I do not believe that was her real name. Her father was a Tory and a volunteer officer with General Howe, so she was often seen about headquarters. She was the most determined flirt on the island,

and never a day passed when she wasn't seen sweethearting with one man or another. My friends, David and Ian, were both smitten with her. The serious, dark-haired David was the one she favored, I think, but I had seen her walking about with merry, fair-haired Ian, too.

David, Ian, and I had grown up in the same Highland village, and we had always been the best of friends. We were foolish rascals in those days, hotheaded and ready to take a dare. Our mothers despaired of us growing to manhood, but somehow we survived our tomfoolery and entered the regiment as soon as we were of an eligible age.

At first, I didn't think Rosie would be a problem. It was obvious to everyone that she was a terrible flirt. Surely David and Ian would not let such a creature destroy a lifelong friendship! But I was wrong. Shortly after I saw Ian and Rosie walking together, David and Ian got into a fight. They made it up the next morning, but later that day I saw Rosie talking with David in the street. I watched as Ian passed the couple, and he refused to answer when Rosie called out to him. The look on his face sent a chill up my spine.

From that moment on, Ian and David were enemies. They each tried to outdo the other in their wooing of Rosie. Flowers, gifts they could ill afford, love poetry, and music were all part of the arsenal they used to win the fair maiden. To no avail. Rosie encouraged each of them, smiling first upon David and then upon Ian with equal favor. But she also smiled on several other men in the regiment. After many futile efforts at reconciliation, I stayed aloof from their feud. I refused to side with either of them and to their credit, each remained my friend.

There was a particularly trying day when Rosie decided to try her tricks on me. She caught me walking down the road and very prettily asked me to escort her to a local entertainment. I refused as politely as I could, but when she pressed the matter, I told her exactly what I thought of her flirtatious ways and refused to have anything to do with her. Rosie hated me for my frankness. She tried to turn David and Ian against me, but I was the one topic on which she could not sway them. They knew I could be trusted and would not betray them.

There finally came a night when David and Ian could stand it no more. David issued a formal challenge to Ian to meet him the next day in the dueling hollow just southwest of the town of New Dorf. I tried to talk them out of the duel, but they were as hotheaded as they ever had been and would not listen to me. I refused to be a second to either of them, and once again they did not think ill of me for not supporting one or the other in the feud. This made me feel worse, if that was possible. I forced a doctor to accompany me to the dueling hollow, fearing for the lives of my friends.

They were just pacing off when we arrived. They took their pistols in hand and fired when the command was given. Ian and David both dropped to the ground, blood staining the red coats of their military uniforms. The doctor and I sprinted over to them. David was closest. I knelt beside him for a moment and saw that he was mortally wounded—shot through the heart. He smiled weakly up at me, murmured Rosie's name, and died before I could say a word to him. I stared in shock at his dead face and then ran over to where Ian lay. The men moved aside so the doctor and I could reach

him. I saw at once that Ian was dead. He must have died instantly.

With the help of the men in my regiment, we carried my friends' bodies back to Richmond Town. I caught a glimpse of Rosie, watching from the side of the road as we carried their bodies through the town. Her pretty face was blank. *Did she feel any remorse at the death of her two suitors?* I wondered angrily. If I were not a Christian man, I would have shot her right then and there for destroying two lives with her flirtatious ways.

We buried David and Ian at the church in unmarked graves, since none of us had the money for a monument. After a small service, we rejoined our regiment and life went on.

I watched Rosie from afar, trying to see some sign of remorse or grief in her. Surely she could not be so cold-blooded as to ignore the deaths of two of her suitors. Yet she continued to flirt with the officers and make merry with their hearts as if nothing had happened. It sickened me.

One evening, a week after the duel, I slipped away to the cemetery to visit my friends' graves. As I approached in the twilight, I saw a slender figure, dressed in gray, planting flowers over the two unmarked mounds. It was Rosie. She was crying as she dug into the earth, silent tears rolling down her cheeks. I stood silently, watching her as she completed her work. She brushed away the tears at last, leaving a smudge on her cheek, and walked away into the gathering twilight, her shoulders slumped.

At that moment I realized how very young she was. It must be terrible to be so young and know you are responsible

THE GRAY LADY

for the deaths of two good men. Not that I excused her in any way, but for the first time, I pitied her.

The war continued, and more mounds joined those of David and Ian in the cemetery. Rosie was still the belle of Richmond Town, but she had lost the pink bloom in her cheeks that had given her the nickname "Rosie." Almost a year to the day of the duel, she succumbed to pneumonia, and her body was interred in the cemetery, not far from David and Ian.

Shortly after her death, the figure of a gray lady began to appear each evening in the graveyard. She would walk among the soldiers' graves before standing over the mounds that covered the bodies of David and Ian. Then she would kneel beside the graves, silver tears coursing down her face, each tear shining brightly in the twilight. The townsfolk claimed the ghost looked just like Rosie, but I never went to see for myself.

4

Redemption

I watched them from the upper window as they played games in the yard. They never seemed to see me, the mother or the father. They were young, caught up in their own lives and concerns, and did not have time for an old German man who did not speak English as well as he should. But their little boy saw me. He looked up and waved cheerfully to me, and his mother asked who he was waving to. "My friend," he said, pointing at me. She looked up at the window and her gaze went straight through me. She turned away and I sighed. Only children seem to notice what is really there. Adults are too busy to see.

I liked this new family who lived in my old home. The father was an honest man who loved his wife and son. He took good care of them, as I once took good care of my wife and son. The mother was charming and intelligent, a fine companion for him. But it was their little boy whom I loved. He was so much like my son who died so many years ago. The boy and I talked and laughed together. He liked my jokes and tried to imitate my German accent.

One night, he asked me to tell him a bedtime story. I

remembered the old folktales my mother used to tell me and so I sat beside his bed and told him of a goose girl who became a queen. The little boy listened with wide eyes, and wanted me to tell him another, just as I had done when my mother finished a tale. I told the boy what my mother told me: "Only one story per night, *mein Kind*. Tomorrow I will tell you another tale."

I watched from the door as he fell asleep. Many nights, my wife and I had stood in this very doorway watching our son as he slept. I walked away slowly, thinking about my wife. I loved her more than I loved my own life, and when she died, she took the best pieces of me with her. The death of my only son had created a hole in my heart; the death of my wife had destroyed my life completely. I couldn't eat. I couldn't sleep. I couldn't care for myself at all. I just sat in my chair day after day, until life faded from my body. But my soul remained behind, trapped in this house and yard.

Almost every night thereafter, I would tell the boy a new folktale from my homeland. Sometimes I would hear him relating the stories to his mother and father the next day. They were always amazed by his tales and did not know where he had learned them, even though they had been sharing the house with me from the day they moved in.

I sometimes wondered if I would always live in this house. I wanted so badly to be with my wife, but my spirit could never reach her, no matter how often I tried to leave. I was trapped here, and even the company of the nice family and their little boy was not enough to assuage my soul. Had my spirit remained here, I wondered, because I had given up at the end instead of trying to go on? I knew the doctrines of my church taught that God does not condone suicide. Or perhaps it was because I wanted my wife more than I wanted anything else, and God was punishing me by keeping us apart.

One night after I finished my story, I stood at the boy's window, thinking about my wife as I gazed up at the stars. I do not know how much time had passed when I saw a flickering light from the ground-floor window of the apartment building behind the house. I went outside to take a closer look, and I saw that the building was on fire.

I ran to the parents bedroom and tried to shake the father awake, but my hands went right through him. He sighed and turned over, but did not wake up. The mother did not stir when I called her name, and I knew the only hope for the two girls who lived in the apartment above the fire was my little friend. I went to the boy, woke him gently, and told him about the fire. He got up at once and went to rouse his parents. They protested a little, but the boy was persuasive, and his father went out to the yard to check on the apartment building. I followed him and watched him gasp in alarm when he saw the fire and hurry to give warning.

Later, when everyone was safe and the fire was out, I stood in the yard looking up at the little boy's window. He was watching the action in wide-eyed excitement, happy to have been the one who had saved the day. When he saw me, he waved. I waved back, hardly aware yet that the yard was becoming misty around me as a beautiful white light illuminated the scene. It was the look on the little boy's face that alerted me. I turned and saw my wife standing a few feet from

REDEMPTION

me. Behind her, I caught a glimpse of a beautiful country full of light and laughter and love. She held out her hand to me, and I stepped forward and took it. I was smiling so hard my face felt sore, but I didn't care about that, any more than I was worried about the tears rolling down my cheeks. We both turned to wave to the little boy. Then we stepped forward into the light and did not look back.

5

The Central Park Skaters

MANHATTAN

I couldn't believe my luck when I got Amy's phone number. We had met at a party, and I was amazed that this woman who resembled a Greek goddess was still single. Amy lived out in the suburbs, and for the first few dates, I drove out there to take her to dinner and the movies. Amy didn't have a lot to say for herself, but she was beautiful, so I kept up my pursuit.

Amy was an old-fashioned kind of girl. We didn't hold hands until our second date, and on the third I was allowed to kiss her cheek. I was hankering to get my arm around her on our fourth date, so I plotted and schemed until I came up with a solution that should appeal to an old-fashioned girl. I would take Amy ice-skating in Central Park. It was time to bring her into my big-city world.

When I called her, Amy seemed a bit reluctant, admitting frankly that she didn't know how to ice-skate. She was amenable to the idea though, until I mentioned coming into the city. You would have thought I had proposed trekking into the jungles of the Amazon. To Amy's mind, Manhattan was populated with the worst sorts of criminals, just lying in wait for a sweet suburban woman to set foot upon its streets. At last I got her to agree to meet me in the city, but she became so agitated about traveling from the bus station to my apartment building that, jokingly, I almost offered to send a bulletproof car and an armed guard to escort her to my door. I held my tongue though, since I suspected she'd take me seriously and not see the humor in my suggestion. I volunteered to meet her bus. This placated Amy, and our conversation ended amiably.

On Saturday I waited patiently for the occupants of the bus to exit at Port Authority, hoping to spot Amy before too long. I noticed a passenger whose garb reminded me of a bag lady, but after a moment I realized the unusually dressed woman was in fact Amy. It was a wonder she could move, muffled as she was from head to toe in so many layers of winter clothing. *At least she won't have to worry about muggers,* I thought cynically. *A bullet would never make it through all that clothing.*

I reluctantly went forward to claim my refugee from the Antarctic and headed downstairs to grab a taxi. I quickly became aware of one of the advantages of bringing a suburban woman to the city. Amy found it necessary to cling closely to me so that I could protect her from all persons of evil intent (everyone from the lady selling flowers to the man sweeping the floors). As Amy had not only the looks but the figure of a Greek goddess, I found her clinging to be a rewarding experience.

Amy was horrified when she learned we were to take a taxi to our destination. Apparently, riding in a taxi in New York City was synonymous with death in Amy's vocabulary. I was prepared for this and kindly suggested that we take the subway. Amy chose the cab.

At one point in our ride, Amy let out a shriek and nearly took off my nose pointing to a large object out the window. "What is that?" she cried.

"That's a horse," I said calmly, "and a carriage. Don't you have horses in the suburbs?"

Amy bristled. "Of course we do," she said briskly, but there was a note of uncertainty in her voice, and I saw the taxi driver suppressing a smile. The horse looked a bit like my Uncle Hubert, but I didn't mention this to Amy, feeling again that my sense of humor might be lost on her.

"I just wasn't expecting to see one in the city," Amy explained with dignity.

I paid the taxi driver and took Amy over to the Wollman Ice Rink to rent ice skates. I had mentally rated Amy's ice-skating potential as somewhere around a negative five (like her IQ, a wicked voice murmured in my head). I found that I had over-estimated her ability. We wobbled around the ice a few times, with Amy clinging to me so tightly that I nearly fell over. I couldn't get her to relax her grip. My arm was starting to go numb due to lack of circulation. *I should,* I thought grimly, *have taken her to a horror film. That would have been a much easier way to get my arm around her.*

Suddenly, my eye was caught by a woman in an old-fashioned, long purple dress. She was skating figure eights on the ice, laughing and obviously enjoying herself. I wondered why she was skating in costume. I didn't see any movie cameras around. She was joined by another woman similarly dressed in a green dress with a long, red velvet coat. They skated around and around, making figure eights on the ice, obviously enjoying the lovely day. I felt quite envious, as Amy and I plod-ded along at the edge of the ice. Amy was whimpering unhap-pily to herself. Really, there was no pleasing this woman.

We turned the bend and found ourselves face to face with the woman in purple. With a quickening of my pulse, I realized that her feet were not touching the ice. And I could dimly make out the figures of other skaters right through her body. She was a ghost!

I must have gasped aloud, because Amy looked up from the careful study of her feet and saw the woman skating toward us. We were on a collision course, and Amy gave a small shriek as the woman skated right through us. For a moment, all I could feel was an ice-cold mist moving through my body. Then it was gone. Amy gave a scream that could have awakened the dead, stumbled over her own feet, and we both fell onto the ice. I rolled over quickly to gaze after the ghost. The woman in purple paused in the middle of her figure eight to look at us lying on the ice. The woman in red stopped beside her, and they both laughed silently at the spectacle we made. Then they disappeared.

A crowd was converging upon Amy and me. We were picked up, dusted off, and a hysterical Amy was helped over to the side of the rink. Somehow, I got her skates off and flagged down a cab to take us back to Port Authority, since Amy refused to stay a moment longer in the big, bad city with its muggers and ice-skating ghosts. I was feeling a bit shaky myself, and I was annoyed that Amy couldn't see how amazing it was that we had both seen a ghost. Also, she was ruining my careful plans. I had dinner reservations at an especially nice

THE CENTRAL PARK SKATERS

restaurant and had intended to spend the whole evening with her.

I saw her onto the bus, and then went home to eat takeout and watch a couple of action-adventure films to soothe my bruised feelings. Amy called the next morning, apologized prettily, and invited me to have dinner with her family that evening. I was still feeling grumpy but decided to give her one more chance, so I agreed.

That afternoon, I went back to the ice rink to talk to some of the regulars. They weren't surprised that I had seen a ghost. Apparently, the lady in red and the lady in purple were sisters. Rosetta and Janet Van der Voort lived in Manhattan during the 1800s. They spent much of each winter ice-skating and loved to draw figure eights on the ice. For Janet's thirty-fifth birthday, they threw a gala ice-skating party in Central Park with a feast spread on long tables and fireworks in the night sky. That evening, the sisters skated in the park with their friends, Janet wearing the purple velvet dress in which I had seen her, and Rosetta in a green dress with a red velvet coat. Both sisters had died in the 1880s, and their ghosts had been seen in Central Park since World War I. Usually, I was told, they appeared on the ice at night, but a few folks besides me had seen them in the late afternoon. I was fascinated. I spent the afternoon skating around the ice, hoping to see Rosetta and Janet again, but they didn't appear.

That evening, I drove to the suburbs to meet Amy's family. I quickly discovered that Amy was not the only family member to resemble a figure in Greek mythology. Her mother was a dead ringer, both in appearance and temperament, for Medusa, the Greek gorgon who had snakes for hair and a dreadful face, and whose gaze could turn men to stone. My father always told me that as women grew older, they started resembling their mothers. But surely Amy would never become so grim-faced and bossy! Then I happened to catch a glimpse of her parents' wedding photo. I could see at once that Amy looked exactly like the younger version of her mother. That decided me. I wasn't taking any chances. I made up a job offer in New Zealand, and that was the last I saw of Amy.

But I am still hoping to see the ghosts one more time.

6

Buried Treasure

LIBERTY ISLAND

For more than a century after that old rascal Captain Kidd was hanged for his pirating and thieving ways, a rumor of buried treasure circulated throughout New York City. This rumor was that the wily captain had actually interred some of his treasure on nearby Bedloe Island. These days, we call this island Liberty Island because the mighty Lady of Liberty graces her shores, but in those days, it was called Bedloe Island, and it had a military fort on it.

The rumor of buried treasure happened to reach the ears of one Sergeant Gibb, who was stationed at Fort Wood, located on Bedloe Island. Gibb, a heavy-set soldier with a broken nose and craggy face, fancied the idea of buried treasure. Being a canny fellow, he instantly came up with a plan for obtaining said treasure. He confided his thoughts to one Private Carpenter, a slender, foxy-faced chap, who was quite enthusiastic both in his praise of the intelligence of Gibb and in the notion of buried treasure.

Together, the sergeant and the private paid a visit to a renowned psychic in New York City. After some preliminary

remarks and exchange of money, the psychic informed the two soldiers that Kidd's buried treasure was located under the largest flat rock on Bedloe Island. "The best way to find the treasure," the psychic said, "is to use a divining rod made of witch hazel under the light of the full moon. When the rod dips toward the ground, it will be pointing to the hiding place of Kidd's treasure!"

Gibb and Carpenter waited eagerly for the next full moon. When the fort had quieted for the night, the two treasure hunters, armed with the witch-hazel divining rod and shovels, made their way north to the large, flat rock they had located earlier. The waves quietly lapped the shore and a path of moonlight glittered across the waters, lighting their way. Gibb carried the divining rod out in front of him, walking forward slowly but steadily toward the flat rock. Carpenter followed impatiently behind him with the shovels, whispering eager questions and stumbling over his own feet in his haste.

Suddenly, the divining rod quivered in Gibb's hands. The sergeant tensed with excitement. He took a careful step forward and the rod dipped down toward the ground. He stopped abruptly and Carpenter bumped into his back. The private gave a startled yelp. "What did you stop for?" he demanded. Then Carpenter saw the divining rod pointing at the ground. He gave a second yelp—this time of joy—and pushed the sergeant to one side. Carpenter thrust the tip of his shovel into the ground where the rod had pointed. Gibb dropped the divining rod and grabbed the second shovel.

The two men dug quickly through the loose sand and earth, aided by the bright moonlight. They were only a few feet deep when their shovels struck something hard. They brushed aside the dirt and gazed down upon the top of a chest about 4 feet in length. Eagerly, they began loosening the dirt from around the chest. Then Gibb's shovel hit something solid buried beside the chest. He swept the dirt away from the object and found himself eye to eye socket with a skull. Gibb gasped in fright and stepped back, bumping into Carpenter. The private turned irritably toward him and saw the skull. He gave a cackle of laughter. "Who do you suppose that was?" he asked. "One of the pirates Kidd killed to guard his treasure and scare people away from his loot?"

As he spoke, the air at the bottom of the hole began to shimmer in the moonlight, and there was a buildup of energy around the two men, making their hair stand on end. A brilliant flash burst from the earth around the chest, flinging the two men out of the hole. A terrible figure rose from the ground where Gibb had disturbed the skull. Its eyes were blazing with an unearthly light that dimmed the glow of the moon. It wore the tattered garb of a sailor with a cutlass at its side, and it clutched a black flag in skeleton hands—the Jolly Roger with its skull and crossed bones. Blue flames poured from its mouth as the ghost uttered a shriek of rage at being disturbed from its slumber. It pointed its cutlass at the two men, moving slowly toward them.

Gibb and Carpenter gave an answering shriek that might have awakened the dead if they had not already done so. Gibb flung himself away from the menacing apparition, tripped over a stone, and landed unconscious in a pool of water. Carpenter ran in the opposite direction, toward the fort, and bumped

BURIED TREASURE

into the night guardsmen, who were coming to investigate all the shouting.

After hearing his garbled tale, the guardsmen marched Carpenter back to the hole he had dug. The hole was there, but the treasure chest and the apparition were gone. The guards found poor Gibb and rescued him from the pool of water before he drowned. Then they escorted the two men back to the fort, where they were reprimanded for being outside the fort without permission.

Ever afterward, Gibb and Carpenter would tell people their tale of the ghost and the buried treasure, pointing out the large, flat rock on the north side of Bedloe Island to verify their story. But the chest and its dead protector disappeared after that night, and no one digging by the flat rock has ever found anything but dirt and sand from that day to this.

7

The Fire Ship

LONG ISLAND SOUND

The crew was busy loading crates of expensive furs into the hold of a merchant ship as she gently rocked at her mooring in Pelham Bay. While the passengers boarded, the ship's captain spoke anxiously to a local member of the watch, seeking the latest news of pirates. There had been no local sightings for over a month, the watchman told the captain. Good news, indeed, but it did little to assuage his uneasiness. There were hundreds of inlets and coves in the sound, and a pirate ship could easily pass unnoticed in one of them.

Governor Peter Stuyvesant had a difficult time keeping the waters of Long Island Sound safe for merchant sailing vessels. Even with a team of forty men watching the waters day and night for signs of pirate activity, many buccaneers still attacked ships, sometimes leaving whole crews dead before slipping silently away in the night.

The captain watched as a beautiful white horse was led aboard his vessel, the last of the cargo. The horse was to be delivered to one of the harbors farther down the Long Island Sound. Then the captain made his way slowly onto the ship and ordered the crew to depart from Pelham Bay. He dreaded this trip, though he had made it more than a hundred times before. He had a premonition of danger that seemed at odds with the cloudless blue sky and the sunlight sparkling on the waters of the bay. He told himself he was being ridiculous. Nonetheless, the captain instructed his crew to keep a wary eye out for pirates. He did not want to take any chances.

It was a perfect day for sailing, with a steady wind, and the crew was in good spirits as they moved out of the bay. The ship seemed to dance over the waves, and the horse, tethered on the deck, neighed and shook his beautiful white mane, turning his face into the warm breeze. The passengers sat on the bales of straw set out for them on deck, laughing and playing cards and calling to the crew as they passed on their various errands. The captain stood watching with an eagle eye, unable to join in the merriment. He shivered in the warm sun, his foreboding growing as they slipped farther and farther from the shores of the bay.

The day was drifting to a close, and the sun was setting in a blaze of glory when the captain spotted a ship sailing toward them. A moment later the first mate sang out a warning, and the captain ordered the passengers below deck as the crew armed themselves. The other ship was sailing quickly, and the captain just knew something was amiss. After several tense moments, the captain could see armed men standing on the deck, grinning viciously at them. The pirate captain on the approaching ship bellowed, "Surrender the ship!" across the rapidly decreasing gap dividing them.

The captain nodded to his first mate, who sent a warning

shot across the bow of the pirate ship. The pirate crew laughed derisively. "Is that the best you can do?" shouted a jeering one-eyed buccaneer, as he caught a heavy grappling hook in one hand and swung it around. He tossed the hook across the water, and it landed on the rail of the merchant ship.

The captain ordered his men to fight. The crew fired their guns again and again at the pirates, pausing only to reload as more grappling hooks caught the rail of the merchant ship and the two vessels came together. The pirate crew leaped onto the deck of the merchant ship and a terrible fight ensued. The captain quickly found himself face to face with his pirate counterpart, and they dueled up and down the deck, slipping in the spilled blood of their crewmen as they fought. Then a buccaneer grabbed the captain from behind and held him tightly as the pirate captain stabbed him through the heart with his cutlass. The captain fell dead onto the deck of his ship, the last member of the crew to die. Then the pirates slaughtered the passengers down in the hold. When all were dead, the pirates removed the expensive furs from the hold and stole the jewelry right off the bodies of the passengers. They even tried to bring the white horse over to their ship, but he reared and bucked and neighed violently, so they tied him to the mast and set fire to the ship before leaping into their own vessel and sailing away.

Behind them, the merchant ship burned and burned in the growing twilight, the white horse screaming and tugging against the ropes that bound him to the mast, his voice nearly human in its agony and fear. None of the pirates looked back at the fiery monstrosity they had created.

Aboard the merchant ship the fire raged uncontrollably, but something strange was happening: Although the flames were fierce, the ship remained intact. In fact, the longer the fire burned, the better the ship looked, her torn sails mending themselves and her blood-soaked decks clean once more.

One by one the passengers, the crew, and finally the captain revived. They stood erect amid the inferno and slowly, soundlessly began going about their usual business. The captain resumed his place near the bow of the ship and watched the dark waters of the sound with an eagle eye. The crew grasped burning ropes and raised the fiery sails. The passengers sat on flaming bales of straw and gambled merrily amongst themselves. No one spoke. No sound could be heard, save for the dreadful neighing of the white horse.

A wild storm had arisen over the sound while the merchant ship burned. As lightning flashed and thunder rumbled in the sky, the fiery merchant ship began to sail forward, following the pirate ship that had set her aflame. It dipped down into the rain-thrashed waves and careened wildly back and forth over the seething water as it pursued the pirates. At first, the buccaneers were too involved in fighting the storm to notice the burning, flickering light sailing toward them through the rain. Then the lookout gave a great shout of terror, almost falling from his post in his fear. The pirates turned as one and saw the burning ship sailing erratically toward them, her silent crew burning right along with the ship, yet not consumed by the flames. The buccaneers were terrified. The pirate captain ordered his crew to flee, and they tried to outrun the terrible, burning ship. They sped madly through the storm-tossed

THE FIRE SHIP

waves and driving rain, their frantic shouts mingling with the rumble of thunder and the neighing of the horse, which was the only sound to be heard from the ship. Some of the hardened pirates even dropped to their knees on the rain-soaked deck and begged God to spare them. But still the ship sailed on, zigzagging crazily through the mighty storm, rolling with the waves of the Long Island Sound and drawing ever closer to the pirates.

Finally, the pirate captain steered his ship into a small, hidden cove, and the merchant ship lumbered past their hiding place and disappeared into the storm. As soon as it was out of sight, the pirates abandoned their ship, leaving it for the authorities to find. Afraid the burning vessel would find them if they stayed in the sound, the pirates stole another ship and sailed out upon the Atlantic to seek their fortunes elsewhere. They never returned.

They say on stormy nights the fiery merchant ship still sails up and down the Long Island Sound, searching for the pirates that set her aflame. In silence, her captain and crew tend to their tasks while the passengers gamble. The only sound is the neighing of a great white horse as it paws the deck and tries to free itself from the mast.

8

Observatory

EMPIRE STATE BUILDING, MANHATTAN

My cousin Julia, a pretty girl in her twenties, had never been to the top of the Empire State Building at night. When she came for a visit to our apartment in Manhattan, my husband, John, and I took her out to dinner and then we all went up to the observatory to look out over the city. It was a clear, still night and we could see for miles. Julia was enthralled with the view from the outdoor promenade. She kept moving from one side to the next, taking deep breaths of the night air and chattering happily to John.

I slipped quietly away to the ladies' room inside the building. Washing my hands afterward, I noticed a young woman wearing a forties' style dress and gloves on her hands. She was weeping softly in a corner of the bathroom. She must have sensed my gaze upon her, for she looked up and quickly wiped the tears from her cheeks. Lifting her chin a little as if defying me to comment on her sadness, she came quickly over to the sink and began applying bright red lipstick to her lips. I debated with myself whether I should speak to her as I dried my hands. But she was the one who spoke first. "We were going to be married," she said to her reflection in the mirror. "We'd known each other since we were kids."

Good lord, I thought. *She's lost her fiancé. Was he dead? Or did he throw her over for someone else?*

"What happened?" I asked her.

"He was killed in the war," she replied, carefully replacing the cap on her lipstick and putting it into her bag.

The war? I thought.

"Which war?" I asked the woman.

She turned abruptly away from the mirror and walked out of the bathroom without looking at me. I blinked in surprise. *That was rude,* I thought. *I wasn't even the one who started the conversation.*

I followed her out the door but did not see where she had gone. I was a bit surprised. She hadn't had much time to disappear so completely. I shivered a bit, suddenly cold. I hurried outside to find John and Julia. They were standing by the barrier at the edge of the promenade, and John was happily pointing out the various sights to Julia. As I joined them, I saw the young woman from the bathroom standing beside two older women. She was wringing her hands, and I thought I heard her saying, "He was killed in Germany. We were going to be married, but he was killed."

Her friends should take her home, I thought, frowning at the two older women. *She is distraught with grief.*

"There you are!" John greeted me heartily, catching my hand in his and giving me a brief kiss on the lips. "We were wondering where you'd disappeared to."

"I just needed to use the ladies' room," I told him, smiling a little and distracted by thoughts of the troubled woman.

Julia bounced up and down on her toes. "This is absolutely marvelous. John was showing me the 59th Street Bridge! The views are magnificent . . ."

Her voice trailed off abruptly and she gasped. John and I turned to look and saw the young woman from the bathroom trying to climb the observatory fence.

"Here! Get down from there!" John shouted, running towards her. Julia and I were hard on his heels. I silently cursed the two women for not taking their young friend home. It was a good thing the fence stood between her and the edge, or she would probably jump.

Then I saw the young woman melt right through the barrier and fling herself off the side of the building. I gasped, Julia screamed, and John let out a yell of pure terror. He slid to a halt beside the barrier and gazed down at the falling figure. I stopped beside my husband and clutched his hand tightly as we watched the girl fall. About halfway down, she vanished into thin air.

The guard came running over to us, wanting to know why we were upsetting the other visitors with our screams. Julia caught his arm in a death grip and frantically tried to explain about the girl who had thrown herself from the observation deck. She wasn't making much sense, so John took over the narrative, carefully describing what we had seen. He hesitated when he got to the part about the woman going through the barrier instead of over it. John liked cold, hard facts. Mysterious things made him uneasy. So I told the guard that the woman had walked right through the barrier as if it didn't exist. "Then she flung herself off the building," I finished, trying to keep my voice steady. I was shaking like a leaf, and I wouldn't let go of John's hand. "Halfway down the building she vanished into thin air, almost as if she were a ghost."

"She was," said the guard solemnly. The three of us stared at him, shocked by his statement. "At least, that's what I have heard. You are not the first visitors to see a young woman throw herself through the barrier and off the building. Was she wearing forties' style clothing and red lipstick?"

"That's her," I said immediately. "I met her in the bathroom."

"Yes, that's consistent with the stories I've heard," said the guard. "Sometimes the ghost appears in the bathroom and puts on her red lipstick, and sometimes she flings herself off the observation deck."

"Do you know who she is? I mean was?" asked Julia.

"Visitors have heard her saying that she lost her fiancé in the war. She claims he was killed in Germany."

I nodded. "That's what she said in the bathroom."

"Germany in the 1940s," said John. "Sounds like World War II."

"Yes, that's what I reckon," said the guard. "But no one knows for sure. Say, are you folks going to be all right? Seeing the ghost jump like that must have been quite a shock."

"I don't know about the rest of you," I said, "but I could use a stiff drink."

John and Julia agreed. The guard escorted us off the observation deck and called the elevator for us, mentioning the name of a good bar that was close by. After a few drinks, we

OBSERVATORY

had all calmed down enough to go back to our apartment.

The next day, as she was leaving for home, Julia said to John and me, "Thanks so much for letting me stay with you this weekend. I really enjoyed dinner last night, and the view from the observation deck of the Empire State Building was absolutely marvelous. I just have one favor to ask."

"What favor?" I queried suspiciously.

"Next time I come for a visit," Julia said, "let's go somewhere that doesn't have a ghost."

9

The Rising of
Gouverneur Morris

Mistress Anne Morris sat on a couch near the fire, watching the flames flicker and listening to the sounds of the wind and the rain whipping against the house. Her three-year-old son was sitting on the floor by the window, playing with his toys and chattering softly to himself. Occasionally he would look up and smile at his mother, and she would try to smile back at him.

She pulled restlessly at her black-edged handkerchief, trying not to weep as she gazed at the portrait of her handsome husband, Gouverneur, and thought of the many times she had sat in this room with him on just such blustery nights, while their son played nearby. Now he was gone, and little Gouverneur would grow up without his father, without the influence of the handsome, witty, fashionable, intelligent man who had sired him.

It would be up to her to make sure that her son knew what a splendid man his father had been. Gouverneur Morris had

51

been born in this very house in 1752, the only son of his father's second marriage. The Morris family was wealthy, and Gouverneur had attended local preparatory schools and then enrolled at King's College at the age of twelve. He had, Gouverneur once told Anne, been both the most intelligent and the laziest boy in school! She had laughed with him at the description. Then, when he was fourteen, he had accidentally upset a kettle of boiling water on his right side, burning his arm so badly that the doctor feared gangrene. His arm was saved, but he bore the scars all his life, and his arm was never much use after that. Anne pressed her lips tightly together to stop them from trembling as she remembered the feel of Gouverneur's withered arm wrapped lovingly around her. His scars had never mattered to her.

She jumped at the sound of little Gouverneur's blocks toppling to the floor. He looked up at her with a happy smile, proud of the noise he had made. She smiled back, catching her breath because his smile was so like his father's. When the child turned back to his blocks, Anne lapsed again into her thoughts of her dear husband.

Gouverneur had gone on to law school and then was admitted to the bar after three years of study with one of New York's leading legal minds. His political career began in 1775, when he took a seat in New York's Revolutionary Provincial Congress, representing Westchester County. In 1776 he joined one of the special militia companies proliferating in New York City. These units acted as the city's Minutemen. *Joining the Minutemen was so typical of Gouverneur,* Anne thought to herself. As a legislator, he was automatically exempted from militia duty, but he had always viewed active service as a moral obligation and insisted on joining the militia in spite of his withered arm.

Gouverneur had excelled as a member of the Provincial Congress. He helped transform the New York colony into an independent state, and the new state constitution was largely his work. He became chairman of the legislature's Ways and Means Committee, which was charged with funding the state's war effort. In May 1776, at the age of twenty-four, the state picked Gouverneur to coordinate defense measures with both George Washington's main army and the Continental Congress.

Then, in the late summer and early fall of the same year, the British invaded New York City and overran much of Westchester County. Gouverneur had not spoken much of this period of time to his wife, but Anne had learned that Mistress Morris, Gouverneur's mother, was a Loyalist who had turned the family estate over to the enemy for military use, and Gouverneur had withdrawn with the Provincial Congress to Fishkill.

Anne's thoughts were interrupted by the chiming of the clock as it struck nine. A light knock sounded on the sitting room door. She bade the person to enter, and her son's French nursemaid came into the room.

"Would you like me to take the child now, Madame Morris?" the girl asked.

"I will keep him here with me," Anne said. "I will put him to bed tonight, Marie. You will not be needed until morning. Have the servants lock up the house and go to bed."

The girl nodded and departed from the room, closing the door behind her. Little Gouverneur was laughing to himself as he came over to his mother to show her a brightly colored block. Anne admired it, and the little boy squirmed with delight before returning to his toys.

Anne took a sip of her now-cold tea, still thinking about the Revolution. *It was in 1777,* she remembered, *that Gouverneur served as a member of the New York Committee of Safety.* He had visited the northern front in the aftermath of the British capture of Fort Ticonderoga. From there he had coordinated state support of the continentals operating in that area, and then he had journeyed to Washington's headquarters to plead for reinforcements. In 1778, while serving as a delegate to the Continental Congress, Gouverneur was selected to serve on a committee being sent to Valley Forge to coordinate military reforms with George Washington. The pitiful plight of the troops in the snow shocked him, and Gouverneur threw himself into his organizational work, serving as the Continental Army's spokesman in Congress. His support for Washington, Nathaniel Greene, and Frederick von Steuben directly contributed to the success of the training and structural reforms.

Gouverneur's political career was cut short when he was defeated in his bid for reelection to the state assembly in the fall of 1778. So Gouverneur decided to relocate to Philadelphia and resume the practice of law. While he was there, he wrote a series of political essays that were published in the *Pennsylvania Packet* and signed only as "An American."

Gouverneur suffered a personal tragedy in May 1780. He

was mounting a carriage in haste when the horses started up. His left foot was caught in the spokes of the wheel, and his ankle was mangled. The doctor who attended him—his own physician was out of town—removed the leg below the knee. When Gouverneur's doctor returned, he opined that the leg could have been saved.

Gouverneur never complained about the loss of his leg, Anne mused, *except when he slipped on muddy cobblestones. Neither his burnt arm nor his missing limb ever slowed him down—he danced, rode, and sailed all his life.*

Gouverneur was ill for several months following the amputation and remained out of the political limelight until 1781, when he became the principal assistant to the Superintendent of Finance for the United States. In 1787 Gouverneur Morris represented Pennsylvania at the Constitutional Convention in Philadelphia. He was one of the leading figures at the convention, standing in the thick of the decision-making process.

It was Gouverneur, Anne thought proudly, *who was the author of much of the Constitution, including the noble phrases of that document's Preamble. "We the People of the United States, in Order to form a more perfect Union, establish Justice, insure domestic Tranquillity, provide for the common defence, promote the general Welfare, and secure the Blessings of Liberty to ourselves and our Posterity, do ordain and establish this Constitution for the United States of America."*

Gouverneur subsequently left public life for a time to devote his attention to business. He purchased the family home from his half-brother, Lewis, and moved back to New York. In 1789 Gouverneur traveled to France on a business venture. There he encountered the growing dissent of the French people, witnessing firsthand the parading of an unpopular government minister's head on a pike through the streets of Paris and the public vendetta against Marie Antoinette. In spite of the terrible political climate, Gouverneur created quite a stir among the married ladies in Paris. Gouverneur had been an inveterate womanizer during his bachelor years. Witty and fashionably attired, the one-legged Gouverneur Morris had entertained a string of ladies across two continents and had once shared a mistress with Talleyrand, one of the most important diplomats in Europe. Gouverneur had never discussed such things with Anne, of course, but his relatives, who disapproved of her, had made sure she knew about them in detail.

George Washington appointed Gouverneur as Minister to France in 1792 to replace Thomas Jefferson. The outbreaks of terror continued, growing worse and worse, and after two years, the American government recalled Gouverneur from his diplomatic duties. Gouverneur chose to continue his business travels in Europe rather than return to America. When he finally came home in 1799, he was a very wealthy man.

Gouverneur settled into the family manor and became active in the Federalist party, allying himself with his friend Alexander Hamilton. As a private citizen, Gouverneur devoted himself to managing his extensive estates, and in 1807 he was named by the state of New York to head the commission to lay out a street plan for Manhattan.

Anne's thoughts were interrupted by a soft wail from her son. She picked him up, cradling him in her arms, and sat down with him before the fire. Comforted by his mother, lit-

tle Gouverneur curled against Anne and fell asleep. She kissed
the top of his head, filled with a sudden joy in this little life she
had created with his father. This son of hers was a miracle
indeed! She had never expected to marry at all after the scandalous happenings of her youth. Yet, after much adversity, she
had married a man she loved very deeply, and who had given
her status, wealth, and a son.

Gouverneur began writing to Anne sometime in 1808. She
was the daughter of his friend Thomas Mann Randolph of
Tuckahoe, Virginia. When Gouverneur heard that she had fallen
on hard times, he offered to help her in any way he could. Anne
frowned a bit. Fallen on hard times! What an understatement
that was! During their correspondence, Anne had eventually
come to trust Gouverneur and had told him her sad story.

Anne had been born into one of the first families in
Virginia. Although they had little money, she and her sister had
been well educated in French, literature, and music lessons, as
was required by their elevated rank in Virginia society. She had
been engaged to marry Theodorick, the younger brother of
her sister's husband, but her fiancé had died before they could
be wed. Then Anne had discovered she was pregnant. Her
child came early and was stillborn. The family tried to keep the
matter quiet, but scandalous rumors of poison and murder
quickly spread throughout Virginia. Anne was accused of having a child with her sister's husband, Richard, and he was
charged with the murder of the baby. Richard was brought to
trial for the crime and was acquitted. Although Anne was never
brought to trial, the terrible charges continued to haunt her
every move.

She was turned out of her home and moved aimlessly from place to place, seeking work. Her path eventually led to a boarding house in Greenwich Village where, destitute and alone, she eked out a living teaching school. Anne was still a good-looking woman at the age of thirty-five, and her spirit had bent but not broken under adversity. Then, in April 1809, Gouverneur had arrived at her door in a fancy carriage driven by French servants and offered her the position of housekeeper in his home. Gouverneur admired Anne for her intelligence, her fierce courage, and her will to survive. During the months she acted as his housekeeper, he wooed her and won her love. They were married on Christmas Day, to the considerable astonishment of the friends and family who had been invited to Morrisiana for a holiday dinner, and who had never expected the 57-year-old Gouverneur to marry.

Oh, how the family had hated her—and Gouverneur—for this unexpected turn of events! She and Gouverneur had stood before the minister in the midst of a sumptuous setting—neo-classical tapestries, gilded chairs, fancy paintings—and Anne had been married in a worn, faded gown with patches on the elbows. All the time the minister was reading from the *Book of Common Prayer,* Anne had been aware of her new relatives hating her for standing between them and the inheritance of Gouverneur's fortune. They protested greatly, but Gouverneur was prepared for them and took delight in "apologizing" to them for having been impertinent enough to marry for his own pleasure.

Their marriage had been a success from the start. They shared many interests, and Anne traveled throughout western

New York with Gouverneur as he carried out his duties as Chairman of the Board of Canal Commissioners, which was in charge of planning and building the Erie Canal. Gouverneur had long dreamed of a canal system that would connect the Hudson River and Lake Erie, and now his dream was becoming a reality.

Their son, Gouverneur Morris Jr., was born in February 1813, destroying the last hope of Gouverneur's nieces and nephews who had once been his heirs. One of his nephews, David Bayard Ogden, had been particularly vicious, digging up gossip from Virginia and trying to wreck their marriage by insinuating that their child was really the son of a servant with whom Anne was having an affair. He encouraged one of Anne's cousins to write a malicious letter accusing her of bringing disgrace and death to their family. With Gouverneur's understanding and support, Anne had publicly renounced her cousin's filthy accusations, and their marriage was further strengthened by the adversity, much to the chagrin of Gouverneur's family.

And now Gouverneur was dead. He died in November 1816, in the same room in which he had been born, and Anne was alone again except for her small son and the servants. Throughout the funeral she had been aware of the fury and resentment of her husband's relatives as they watched her. Anne hugged her son tightly against her, afraid suddenly of what Gouverneur's family might do to her and her child now that he was not there to protect them.

It was nearly midnight. The servants had all gone to bed, and Anne suddenly became aware of how weary she was. She stood up, cradling her sleeping son, and shivered as she listened to the rain and sleet hitting the window pane. As she moved toward the door of the sitting room, she heard the sound of horses' hooves pounding their way to the front of the house. Anne hurried to the front hallway, wondering what emergency was bringing someone to her home at this late hour. There came a great pounding at the door, and a man's voice shouted, "Anne Morris, fetch us our cousin's will or we will break into the house and take it!"

Anne's eyes widened as she recognized the voice of her husband's cousin. She clutched little Gouverneur tightly to her chest and rang for the servants, hoping someone would hear her summons. The pounding came again, harder this time, and Anne moved back toward the sitting room, determined to lock herself in with her son. But she stopped short, staring at the coat of arms over the door. She thought she had seen it move. She gasped suddenly when one of the lions stretched and shook itself. Around the walls, the portraits began to move, the figures stirring and stretching within their frames as if newly awakened.

Then the figure of a knight leaped down from his frame, alighting on the floor with a clink of armor. Gravely, he struck his shield with his sword three times, the tones ringing forth like a bell through the pounding on the door and the shouts from outside. Anne stared at the ghost in fear and alarm. She did not know if she should be fleeing from him or from the kinsmen who threatened her.

Then the ghost called out in a deep, hollow voice, "Gouverneur Morris! Come forth."

Anne cried out in alarm. Overhead, she heard a footfall in the room where Gouverneur had died, then the familiar thump of a pegleg hitting the floor. Anne stood frozen in place, watching as the ghost of her husband, a sword in his hand, descended the staircase and entered the hallway. The shade of Gouverneur Morris gestured toward the front door with his sword; the door blasted outward, throwing the intruders backward down the stairs. He moved forward without haste, followed by the warrior from the painting, and together the ghosts stepped into the rain and sleet of the cold night, swords raised. Anne heard several voices scream in terror, then the sound of her husband's kinsmen hastily mounting their horses and galloping away.

The front doors closed with a bang, and the light from the candelabrum on the mantel flickered. Anne clutched her still-sleeping son to her chest, wondering if she dared to move. Then Gouverneur, her beloved husband, materialized in front of her, a tender smile on his face. Taking the candelabrum from the mantel, the ghost led his wife from room to room of their mansion, showing her the secret drawers and shelves where he had hidden many of the deeds to his various proper-ties and other important papers, money, and jewels—all the things he had meant to show her before death parted them. He stopped at last beside the fire in the sitting room where they had often sat on just such a blustery night while their son played nearby. Gently, he sat her down beside the fire and stooped as if to kiss her. At that moment, the clock on the mantel struck one, and Gouverneur vanished into his portrait on the wall.

THE RISING OF GOUVERNEUR MORRIS

Anne sat very still, tears coursing down her cheeks as she bade her husband good-bye in her heart. Then she stood, cradling her son in her arms, and went up to bed.

10

Tug-of-War

HALFMOON

Now, my cousin P. S. Woodin is a successful businessman, and he's got a pretty solid head on his shoulders. But when he told me that he owned a haunted house, I told him that he was plumb crazy. It was a nice, redbrick house about a half-mile above the bridge, and it sat right in front of an old Indian burial ground. Woodin had rented out the house more than once, but no one ever stayed there for long.

"I'm telling you, the tenants all claim the house is haunted," Woodin told me. "I'm not making it up. I think maybe it has something to do with that old Indian burial ground in the back."

"I think it has something to do with the quality of the people you rent the house to," I snapped. "Honestly, Woodin, I might believe there were rats in the floorboards, or even squirrels in the attic. But ghosts?"

"Why don't you stay there a few nights?" suggested Woodin. "Check the place out. I won't charge you any rent."

"Charge me rent?" I snapped. "You should pay me for dispelling the rumors. A haunted house!"

I packed a bag that very night and moved into the house. It was a large house and quite comfortable. I put my things away and spent a quiet evening reading a book before I went to bed. I fell asleep almost immediately and was dreaming happily about food when the covers were snatched right off my bed. I woke up at once, blinking blurrily in the darkened room.

"Good gravy, what a terrible draft!" I mumbled, sliding to the floor and picking up the covers. I staggered back to bed with my covers and went back to sleep. I had the top quilt clutched in my hand, the corner tucked under my chin. Suddenly, the quilt was ripped out of my grasp so fiercely that it yanked me halfway down the bed. I snapped awake again.

"You cut that out!" I shouted to the irritating draft. "Honestly, can't a man get some sleep around here?" I fetched my covers, tucked them firmly in around me, and went back to sleep.

The next morning, I carefully examined my room, trying to find the annoying draft that had kept blowing my covers off the night before. The room was well constructed, and there didn't seem to be any gaps around the windows or the door. Still, I decided I was overlooking something, since I knew for a fact that there was no such thing as a ghost.

I went to work that day and forgot all about my interrupted sleep as I immersed myself in the various tasks that crossed my desk. It wasn't until I finished a late supper and went up to my room that I recalled the incident with the blankets.

"Ghosts! Balderdash and poppycock!" I growled, quoting some of the favorite Victorian sayings of the character in the book I was reading. I settled back against the pillows and read for an hour before turning off the light. As I made myself comfortable, the door to the room blew open with an eerie creak. For a moment I had the strange impression that someone had come into the room.

"What nonsense!" I said aloud, and turned over on my side. A moment later, the covers were snatched right off my body.

"Hey!" I shouted, sitting bolt upright. I jumped out of bed and grabbed the quilts from the floor. "I'm going to have to get that draft fixed in the morning," I defiantly told the darkness, climbing back into my bed and tucking the covers firmly about me. I kept the top quilt clutched in both hands and lay waiting for the strange draft to strike again. Nothing happened.

"Nonsense," I muttered, turning over and letting go of the top quilt. I was nearly asleep when the covers were whipped aside, leaving me completely bare. "I do not believe in ghosts!" I shouted, climbing out of bed and grabbing the quilts. I returned to the bed and slept with the covers firmly wrapped around my arms for the rest of the night.

I found it much harder to keep my attention on work the next day. My sleep had been restless, to say the least, since I kept expecting my blankets to be blown off by that strange draft. When I finished work that night, I stopped by the house of a friend who was a carpenter. My buddy cheerfully accompanied me to the house and examined the room for drafts.

"Nothing here," he told me after giving the room a thorough going-over. "It must be your imagination."

I snorted expressively and escorted him out the front door rather more rapidly than necessary. I hated being laughed at.

When I went to bed that night, I tucked each and every cover under the mattress before I got in. Then I lay still, gripping the quilts tightly with both hands. I was unsurprised when the door blew open with an alarming creak, and an invisible presence entered the room. I turned slightly, making the springs of the bed squeak, and started to snore. A few moments later, I felt a hard tug on the covers. I tugged back, equally as hard. That did it! The covers were yanked away so fast I was half lifted off the bed.

"Oh, no, you don't!" I shouted, pulling back so fiercely that the muscles in my arms corded with the strain. I was making progress. The covers advanced slowly toward me, and I rolled myself down onto the bed and pulled the quilts back up to my chin. Suddenly, the blankets were whipped backward so fast I landed facedown on the foot of the bed. The quilts fell with a triumphant thump to the floor. A moment later, the door blew shut with a bang.

"I still don't believe in ghosts," I muttered grumpily, rolling off the bed to retrieve my covers.

The next night, I went into the bedroom with a hammer and several nails and nailed the bedroom door shut. "I'd like to see a draft get through that!" I said, punctuating each word with a strike of my hammer. Was it my imagination, or did the air suddenly get chilly? I shivered. "Rubbish!" I exclaimed, trying to rid myself of the notion that I had angered something . . . or someone.

I felt certain that I would have an undisturbed sleep. Nothing was coming through that door tonight. I drifted off peacefully and was deep in dreamland when the bedroom door crashed open and the covers were snatched off my body so hard they left marks on my bare legs. "Cut that out!" I yelled, jumping to my feet and grabbing the covers from the floor. Immediately, the covers were yanked from my arms. I managed to grab the end of one of the blankets and pulled back, really angry now. Back and forth, back and forth the invisible presence and I wrestled, knocking into furniture, rolling right across the bed, neither of us giving an inch. Finally, I let go of the blanket so suddenly that it snapped backward and I heard a distinct "thump," as if something . . . or someone . . . had fallen to the floor. "Get out!" I shouted at it. I must have won that round in our game of tug-of-war, because the door slammed shut with a rather sulky sound, like a spoiled child denied a toy. "Good night and good riddance," I exclaimed, reclaiming my covers and climbing into bed.

I examined the door in the morning, and I couldn't find a single nail left in place. I couldn't even find the holes where I had driven the nails into the wood the night before. That creeped me out something awful, but "in for a penny, in for a pound" as the saying goes. I was committed to my course, and nothing was going to keep me from making that house habitable, ghost or no ghost.

For three weeks I played tug-of-war each night with the unseen presence in the house. Sometimes, I lay on the bed and just pulled and pulled against the spirit that was trying to deprive me of my covers. Sometimes, we raged back and forth around the room like we did the night I nailed the door shut. But I finally admitted defeat the night the spirit pulled me and the blankets to which I was stubbornly clinging right off the

TUG-OF-WAR

bed. It yanked the blankets straight toward the bedroom window with me sailing along behind them. I let out a yelp and let go of the blankets just as the window opened with a bang and the blankets sailed through. I hit the floor with a terrible thump that shook the floorboards.

I didn't hear a sound, but there was a distinctly triumphant air about the room as I slowly got to my feet. "All right! You win," I said in disgust. "I believe in ghosts. Do you hear me? I BELIEVE IN GHOSTS! Happy now?"

I felt the invisible presence saunter out of the room. It closed the door with a smug creak. I shook my fist at the door, then I turned on the light, packed my bag, and went home. The next morning, Woodin went to the redbrick house, retrieved the quilts from the front lawn, and had them washed, since I refused to go anywhere near that stupid house again.

A few months later, a workman discovered a weathered skeleton near a spring in the back of Woodin's property. My cousin had the skeleton buried, and ever since then, no tenants have complained of a ghost in the house. But I think that is just a lot of balderdash and poppycock. I think that pesky ghost is just waiting for another nonbeliever to sleep in its favorite bedroom so it can play a few more rounds of tug-of-war.

11

Going Fishin'

HERKIMER COUNTY

When folks in town said our new house was haunted, we just laughed. Neither my husband, Tom, nor I believed in ghosts. The house had been abandoned for several years, and my husband said it was just the sort of story that people would invent about a neglected house.

We soon had the place fixed up nicely, and we thought it was just perfect except for one small annoyance. There was a closet under the front stairway with a door that wouldn't stay shut. It had a wooden knob that supposedly secured the door, and when I turned the knob to the closed position and tugged, the door felt solid. But every morning when I came down to make breakfast, the door to the closet was open. At first this was amusing, then irritating, and then it became downright spooky. We had a carpenter take a look at the door, but he could not find anything wrong with it.

I never mentioned my experiences in town, because I knew that everyone would take the open door as proof that the house was haunted. Tom and I discussed the door frequently, and finally he went and bought a chain, which he attached to the door. The next morning, just before dawn, we were awakened from a sound sleep by the loud rattling of the chain. There came a thump, a final rattle, and then silence. We looked at each other, and then we crept cautiously downstairs. The closet door stood open, with the chain dangling forlornly beside it. We searched in vain for the person who had opened the door, but there was no one in the house or the yard. After several mornings of this, Tom rose before dawn and hid himself near the staircase to see who was opening the door. I heard the rattle of the chain and then my husband gave a yell and ran upstairs, lickety-split.

"Honey, the chain rattled itself!" he shouted. "The chain just unlocked itself, the wooden knob turned by itself, and the door opened by itself."

"Are you serious?" I asked suspiciously, thinking he was pulling my leg. Then I realized he was pale and trembling with shock, and he kept running his hands through his dark hair. I knew he was serious.

"We have a ghost in the house," Tom said, sitting down on the bed.

I thought about this for a moment. "Do you mind?" I asked cautiously. Slowly, Tom shook his head. "It doesn't seem to be malicious in any way," he said. "It just wants to get into the closet."

"Well then, we'd better remove the chain and let it get on with whatever it wants to do in the closet," I said briskly. That settled the matter. Tom removed the chain, and each morning I would shut the closet door on my way to make breakfast.

A few weeks after our ghostly discovery, my brother John

came for a visit. An avid fisherman, he rose before dawn on the morning after he arrived and went to the local trout stream near our home. The stream ran through an old mill pond, and John decided to fish near the ruins of the mill. As he approached the pond, my brother saw a man wearing old-fashioned clothing fishing from the bank. The man was seated on a stump and had placed a large stick in the ground in front of him with the fishing pole resting in the fork between two branches.

"Having any luck?" John called jovially to the old man. The fisherman ignored him. "Are the fish biting today?" John tried again, a little louder this time, thinking the old man was hard of hearing. There was no response. John shrugged his shoulders and walked past the fisherman toward a spot farther along the pond.

After a few feet my brother turned to look back at the strange old man. The man had vanished. John stopped in his tracks, startled. The area around the pond was flat, and there had not been time for the old gent to pack up his gear and disappear into the trees at the back of the property. The only place he could have gone was the ruined mill, unless he had walked into the pond. John looked in the water, but he only saw a few fish. Puzzled, he went to the old mill and peered inside. No one was there. Retracing his steps, John paused at the stump where the old man had sat fishing a few moments before. There were no footprints in the soft ground save those John's boots had made as he passed the spot. And there was no hole where the forked stick holding the fishing pole had been sunk into the ground. It gave him goose bumps, John told us later. He thought he must have dreamed the whole thing.

He told Tom and me the story over breakfast, and repeated it later that day when we were in town. Several of the older residents, who were blatantly eavesdropping on us as we sat at the counter of the local diner eating hamburgers for lunch, exclaimed excitedly when John described the old fisherman.

"That's old Mr. Brockhurst who used to live in your house," an ancient man seated beside us said. "He used to fish in that millpond ever day of the year, come rain, snow, or shine. He would hack a hole in the ice in wintertime."

"Must have been his ghost you saw," cackled another old fellow from a booth near the back. "I told you the house was haunted!"

"I didn't see him in the house," John reminded the old men.

"Brockhurst had the most impressive set of fishing tackle I've ever seen," the first man said reminiscently. "He kept it in a small closet under the stairs and would never let anyone touch it."

Tom and I both stiffened when he mentioned the closet. We exchanged glances.

"What happened to Mr. Brockhurst?" I asked.

"He drowned in the millpond one winter. Folks said it was suicide, but I think he just fell through thin ice," the old man said.

"Well, that explains the open door," Tom said to me and John after we'd left the diner. "Brockhurst must be fetching his tackle out of the closet each morning so he can go fishing."

We laughed a bit shakily and agreed with him.

As we passed a sporting goods store on our way to the car,

GOING FISHIN'

John suddenly excused himself and went inside. He came out a few minutes later carrying a shopping bag.

"What did you buy?" asked Tom.

"Some new lures," John said.

This was so typical of John that I laughed. He had brought a mountain of fishing tackle with him and now he was buying more. "Didn't you bring enough fishing gear with you?" I teased him.

"Oh, this isn't for me," said John.

"Who's it for?" I asked curiously.

"This is for Mr. Brockhurst," John said. "He must be tired of using the same tackle over and over again, so I thought I'd leave some new stuff in the closet for him. We fishermen always like to try out new gear!"

Tom and I laughed at his foolishness as we got into the car and drove home.

I was awakened the next morning by a muffled exclamation of delight from downstairs, followed by cheerful whistling. Thinking that John was going fishing again, I turned over and went back to sleep. When I went down a half-hour later to start breakfast, I was surprised to see John standing in the open door to the closet. He was still in his bathrobe and was sipping a hot cup of coffee. John was looking at the empty shelves inside the closet, and I went to peer in the door with him.

"What are we looking at?" I asked.

"Nothing," John said with satisfaction. "I left the new lures on the top shelf last night, and now they're gone!"

I shivered a bit. "Do you think Mr. Brockhurst took them?" I asked.

"He'd better have," John said briskly. "Or I just wasted twenty bucks!"

I felt a bit spooked, looking at the empty shelves where the lures had been. I closed the closet door and hastened into the kitchen to make breakfast, remembering the muffled exclamation and the cheerful whistle I had heard earlier.

Yes, I thought as I broke several eggs into the frying pan, *I believe Mr. Brockhurst did take the new lures with him this morning when he went fishing.*

I was smiling as I turned on the stove and started scrambling eggs for breakfast.

12

The Poker Game

LOWVILLE

Now Maggie was a good wife to me. No one will argue that point. She was pretty and smart, a good cook, had a sweet disposition, and she really seemed to appreciate a man's efforts, which was a very rare thing. If I had to live my life over, I would woo and win her again. But God didn't make anybody perfect, not even Maggie. Her one major flaw was in her attitude toward poker. Maggie did not like gambling at all, no sir, and poker was her pet peeve so to speak.

Since my bachelor days, me and the boys have gathered once a week to play a few hands of poker. We didn't do much gambling, mind you. No one lost his shirt and the stakes remained mighty low. We just had a few beers and a few laughs and played poker 'til round about midnight, when we would wrap things up and head for hearth and home. We all took turns hosting the poker game; all except me, of course. Maggie would never let me invite the boys to our house. We had many parties in our home over the years, so Maggie was well acquainted with my poker buddies, but she wouldn't allow no gambling, and she told them so in no uncertain terms. They

teased me sometimes about who wore the pants in our family, but they knew us too well to think that Maggie totally ruled the roost. It was just on this one point that there was disagreement.

We had shared a lot of years, and our kids were grown with kids of their own when Maggie turned poorly and died within a few months. I was heartbroken, and the house felt big and empty as I rambled around the interior by myself with no Maggie humming in the kitchen or waving to me from the garden when I came home from work. Still, I felt a touch of relief when I realized that I could finally host the poker game at my house when my turn came in the rotating schedule. I waited for about six months, out of respect for Maggie, before inviting my buddies over to the house for a game.

"Seems a bit hard on poor Maggie, us playing here," my friend Patrick remarked as he dealt the cards.

"Seems a bit hard on us that we had to wait until she was dead to come here and play poker, right Matt?" snapped Gil, who was studying his hand with a fierce concentration that meant he had nothing and was going to try to bluff.

"Water under the bridge, boys," I told them. "Maggie is gone now and I won't hear any talk against her."

"Still, it solves the problem of where to play poker every week," Alan remarked.

"What do you mean?" I asked, glancing at him over my cards.

"Some of the wives are getting a might touchy over hosting the game," explained Danny. "I think they'd be happier if we'd just settle in one spot where none of them had to host.

Like here, for example." He gave me a broad wink and lay down the winning hand.

I sent up a mental apology to Maggie's spirit and agreed.

Things went swimmingly for about three weeks. Then Gil phoned me to say he wouldn't be able to come to the poker games any more. He made up some excuse about a new commitment on Thursday nights and rang off before I could grill him. I asked the boys about it when they came that evening, but no one knew anything more than what Gil had told me.

Gil seemed a bit nervous of me when I bumped into him at the hardware store on Saturday. He claimed his wife had volunteered him for a committee that met on Thursday nights. His story sounded rather weak to me, but I didn't press the matter.

The next Thursday, Danny was on the phone canceling for poker night. His wife was feeling poorly, and he couldn't make it. He didn't even bother to phone the following week, he just didn't turn up. Neither did Alan.

"What is going on?" I asked Patrick, the only other member of our poker game to turn up that night.

Patrick looked uneasy. "I ain't sure I should tell you, Matt," he said. "I only heard it secondhand from Danny's wife."

"Heard what?" I asked.

"You know that lonely stretch of road that goes through the swamp? The place where the mists always gather around dusk? Well, Danny was walking home through that spot one night after the poker game, and he saw a light begin swirling in the mist. It stretched up higher and higher, until it took on the form of a woman." Patrick glanced at me nervously. "Danny told his wife it was Maggie."

"Maggie!" I exclaimed in disbelief.

"The ghost told Danny that there was no poker playing in heaven, and that if he did not mend his ways, his soul would be in jeopardy," Patrick said. I groaned aloud. That sounded like Maggie all right.

"Apparently, the same thing happened to Gil and Alan. At least, that's what their wives told my wife. Shook them up pretty bad. They both started volunteering for extra duties at church, and suddenly they are the ones dragging the family out of bed on Sunday morning to go to early Mass."

"Good lord," I exclaimed. "Are you serious?"

"Serious enough not to walk that patch of swamp after dark," said Patrick. He grinned as he spoke, but I knew he wasn't joking. "Serious enough that this is my last poker night."

I stared at him in disbelief. Patrick had played poker practically from infancy.

"Hey Matt, you may be willing to risk your eternal soul," he said, "but I'm not. I figure, if Maggie thought it was important enough to return from the grave to warn us away from poker, then we should do what she says."

He lay down his hand—it was a winner, like always—picked up his coat and hat, and left the house.

"If she thought it was so important," I shouted out the door after him, "how come she never came to warn me?"

Patrick just waved and got into his car.

"Would you have listened to me if I did?" asked Maggie's voice from behind me.

THE POKER GAME

I swung around. Maggie was standing next to the fireplace, beside the poker table, wearing one of her pretty dresses and smiling warmly at me. She looked a lot younger than when I last saw her alive, and her skin glowed a bit from an inner radiance that could not quite be hidden.

"You are such a spoilsport, Maggie," I grumbled, my heart fluttering at the sight of her. She looked just as she had the day I married her, and suddenly I missed her so much I wanted to cry. "Scaring the boys away from poker night. Telling them they are going to lose their souls if they play."

"You don't believe it's true?" Maggie asked me with the mischievous grin I remembered so well from our youth.

"I think you just don't want them playing poker in our house," I accused her, stepping closer to look into her ethereal blue eyes.

"You may be right, Matt," Maggie said. "Then again, you may be wrong!" She stepped forward and kissed me lightly on the mouth, and then she was gone.

I packed up the cards, chips, and table and put them away. Somehow, I didn't think the boys would be back to play poker at my place. Or maybe at any place. I didn't mind as much as I thought. Seeing Maggie again, even if it was just for a moment, made me realize that I had not truly lost her forever. I felt a sense of peace for the first time since she died.

"Still," I said aloud, "isn't it just typical of a woman! If she can't get her way in life, she has to sneak around and get her way after death. Thanks a lot, Maggie!"

For a moment, the house rang with the sound of Maggie's laughter. Then I was alone again.

13

The Galloping Hessian

TARRYTOWN

The soldier was given command of the Prince Hereditaire Regiment just days before they set sail from Germany at the behest of George III, King of Great Britain and ruler of the German principality of Hanover. The British king did not have enough soldiers in his own army to supply the needs of his commanders in America, so he signed a treaty with Frederick II, the Prince of Hesse-Cassel, who often rented out his soldiers in order to make ends meet. The soldier arrived in the American colonies in August 1776.

We are not true mercenaries, the soldier mused as he came ashore his first day in the New World. *We receive no compensation for our services beyond our daily bread. It is our Prince who grows rich from our military skills, not us.*

He must have spoken the last bit aloud, for his friend laughed and said, "That is true, *mein freund,* but let not General Knyphausen hear you say so."

The soldier quickly discovered that the American General, George Washington, was resting on Harlem Heights with the main body of his army. The Americans were watching the movements of the British General Howe from a five-sided earthwork named Fort Washington. The fort was the principal fortification within the American lines, standing 230 feet above tidewater, with strong ravelins and outworks, and thirty-four great guns.

On October 12, General Howe ordered the British troops to land on Throgg's Neck, a low peninsula jutting out from Westchester County. Washington immediately sent forces to oppose the landing, ordering the American troops to occupy lower Westchester. In spite of fierce opposition, the British took post on the heights of New Rochelle, across the road leading to White Plains. It was at this time that the soldier and his regiment, under the command of General Knyphausen, marched to support General Howe, along with a freshly arrived corps of German troops.

To prevent his army from being surrounded by the British, Washington moved all his troops into Westchester save for one garrison ordered to hold Fort Washington at any cost. The American army marched in four divisions, moving up the valley of the Bronx River and forming entrenched camps from the heights of Fordham to White Plains. On October 21 George Washington made his headquarters near the village of White Plains.

On October 28, after almost daily skirmishing, the American and British armies, each about thirteen thousand strong, met in battle array at the village of White Plains. The Americans were encamped behind entrenchments just north of the village, with hills in the rear to retreat to. In addition, nearly sixteen hundred Yankees, with two pieces of artillery under the charge of Captain Alexander Hamilton, had taken post on Chatterton's Hill.

The British army approached the Americans in two divisions, right and left. General Howe inclining his army to the left, planted almost twenty fieldpieces. Under cover of the artillery, the British troops constructed a bridge across the Bronx River and sent British and German battalions to ascend the steep, wooded Chatterton's Hill. The soldier was among the Hessian commanders sent to drive the Americans from the hill. Hamilton's cannon battered at the troops, and the soldier was forced to pull his men back to wait for reinforcements. When they arrived, the soldier led his men in a charge up a gentle slope. The soldier rode directly into a tempest of bullets, one of which drove into the forehead of his horse. Horse and rider fell to the ground together, but the soldier leaped up immediately so his men could see he lived. As he straightened to his full height, a cannonball blew his head from his shoulders and the soldier fell dead to the ground. He did not see his men take the hill and force the Americans to retreat to Washington's camp near White Plains.

Howe decided not attack Washington's entrenched camp without reinforcements. Additional British troops soon came to his aid, but a severe rain storm set in before they could attack, and it raged until twilight on October 31. Washington, perceiving Howe's tactical advantage, withdrew his troops under the cover of darkness toward the Croton River. Howe did not follow. Instead, the British fell back and encamped on the heights of Fordham. After a council of war, Washington decided to retreat into New Jersey with a large portion of the army, leaving the New England troops on the east side of the Hudson to defend the passes in the highlands.

For many days following the battle of White Plains, local residents and the British troops gathered up the dead and buried them. The Hessian soldier's body was discovered on Chatterton's Hill, but no one located his head, and so he was interred headless in the graveyard near Tarrytown.

In the months following the battle, many of the good people living in Tarrytown went out of their way to avoid passing the cemetery after dark. There was something restless about, folks said. Strange lights would appear in the graveyard around midnight, and one woman claimed to have heard the sound of an invisible horse galloping madly down the road. Most people treated the rumors as a funny joke and ignored them. However, a few of the older residents took care to mention a folk belief they had learned in childhood: that evil spirits and ghosts did not care to cross running water. If the spirit haunting the graveyard ever bothered anyone, that person should make for the bridge as fast as his legs would carry him.

One cold winter night, early in the new year, a certain Dutchman named Hans left the tavern in Tarrytown and started walking to his home in the hollow nearby. His path led next to the old cemetery where the Hessian soldier was buried. At midnight, Hans came within site of the graveyard. The weather had warmed up during the week, and the snow was almost gone from the road. It was a dark night with no moon, and the only light came from his lantern and a few remaining patches of snow that sparkled when they caught the light.

Hans was nervous about passing the graveyard, remember-

THE GALLOPING HESSIAN

ing the rumors of a galloping ghost that he had heard at the tavern. He stumbled along, humming to himself to keep up his courage. Suddenly, his eye was caught by a light rising from the ground in the cemetery. He stopped, his heart pounding in fear.

"Who is there?" he called, trying to sound casual. The only response was a whooshing sound as the white mist burst forth from an unmarked grave and formed into a large horse carrying a headless rider.

Hans let out a terrible scream as the horse leaped toward him at a full gallop. He took to his heels, running as fast as he could, making for the bridge where he prayed the fearful apparition would disappear. Hans could hear the pounding of ghostly hooves behind him, and he stumbled suddenly and fell, rolling off the road into a melting patch of snow. The headless rider thundered past him, and Hans got a second look at the headless ghost. It was, he realized, wearing a Hessian commander's uniform.

Hans waited a good hour after the ghost disappeared before crawling out of the bushes and making his way home. After fortifying himself with schnapps, Hans told his wife about the ghost. By noon of the next day, Hans's wife had spread the story all over Tarrytown. The good Dutch folk were divided in their opinions. Some thought that the ghost must be roaming the roads at night in search of its head. Others claimed that the Hessian soldier rose from the grave to lead his men in a charge up Chatterton's Hill, not knowing that the hill had been taken by the British. Whatever his reason, the galloping Hessian continues to roam the roads near Tarrytown on dark nights from that day to this.

14

The Satin Dress

FLUSHING, QUEENS

She worked in a box factory, and her salary was not large. She made just enough to cover the cost of food, shelter, and the clothes on her back. She could barely afford the fare from the factory to her flat in Flushing. So when she received an invitation to a fancy-dress party from an old friend who had married well, she did not know what she should do. Here was her chance at last to shine a little, to experience how the other half lived. She was quite pretty, and she might catch the eye of a rich young bachelor, as her friend had before her. But she had no money to buy a dress, or even to purchase the material to make one.

She mentioned her dilemma to a woman at the box factory. "Why not rent a costume?" the woman suggested. "It shouldn't cost much for just one evening. Try your local pawnshop."

She thought the idea had merit, and so she made her way to a pawnshop near her home after work. At the rear of the store, she found a beautiful satin gown, complete with matching accessories. The owner of the shop was willing to rent the gown to her for a reasonable fee. She decided attending the party was more important than drinking milk, at least for one week, so she paid the fee and took the beautiful gown home with her the night of the party.

She dressed carefully for the occasion and peered at her reflection in the tiny mirror in her bathroom. She looked radiant, her blue eyes glowing with the excitement of an evening out, her pale hair piled high on her head. She patted the satin dress with a white-gloved hand. As she turned away from the mirror, she thought she heard a ghostly voice whisper: "Give me back my dress." She froze in the doorway, looking around uncertainly for the speaker, but saw no one. She shrugged, went downstairs, and splurged on the cab fare into Manhattan.

Her friend greeted her enthusiastically when she arrived, exclaiming in wonder over the beautiful satin dress. She was quickly inundated with dance partners, and the men kept cutting in on each other on the dance floor. She felt like Cinderella at the ball, and the first hour of the party quickly slipped away.

She slowly became aware of growing nausea when she paused to sip some wine between dances. She felt light-headed, and the room was spinning rather faster than the movements of the dance would warrant. For a moment, she heard a ghostly whisper in her ear: "Give me back my dress." She gasped, and her partner apologized, thinking he had stepped on her foot.

She ignored her physical discomfort for a while, trying to smile into the faces of her partners, but finally the nausea overwhelmed her. She gave an excuse to the man with whom she was dancing and slipped away. She made her way to the street and managed to summon a cab to take her home. After paying

THE SATIN DRESS

the fare, she staggered into the building and crawled up the steps to her flat.

It took her a long time to get the key into the lock because her hands were trembling. She fell in the door at last and stumbled brokenly to her bed. As she threw herself onto the covers, she heard a ghostly voice whisper in her ear for the third time: "Give me back my dress."

"Why?" she gasped, as her vision grew dark and pain overwhelmed her.

"You have stolen this dress from the dead," the voice whispered, "and I want it back."

The young woman was found dead the next day, and the circumstances were unusual enough to warrant an autopsy. The report stated that the young woman had been poisoned by embalming fluid, which had entered her pores when she grew overheated from the dancing at the party. The authorities found the receipt for the dress rental and questioned the pawnbroker, who told them he had purchased the dress from a poor undertaker's assistant. The dress that had killed the young woman had been removed from the body of a dead girl just before her casket was nailed shut and buried in the local graveyard.

The undertaker's assistant fled the city when he heard about the young woman's death, and the police were never able to locate him.

15

One Last Drink

NEW YORK CITY

My cousin, Paddy O'Dell, was the hardest drinker in a long line of drinking O'Dells, and that was really saying something. Old Paddy could drink even the toughest Irishmen under the table. I have seen strong men turned pale when my cousin invited them to belly up to the bar with him. Paddy would often drink himself into a stupor and slip down for a rest beneath his favorite table at the local bar in the Five Points neighborhood in lower Manhattan. Then, just when the bartender thought it was safe to throw him out, up he would surface and demand some more Irish whiskey.

Mrs. O'Dell never could raise her head among the good ladies of her church, for all of them knew that her man was drunk from dawn 'til midnight and would probably drink all the other hours, too, if he didn't need to sleep sometimes. He was a friendly drunk and never laid a hand on his wife and kiddies, but he couldn't hold down a job for long, on account of it interfered with his drinking. So Mrs. O'Dell worked at the local grocery to support the family.

Yes, the church ladies pitied Mrs. O'Dell and often called

at the house to console her, daintily ignoring the loud snores coming from the bedroom upstairs. Oddly enough, the young O'Dells rarely touched liquor, maybe because Paddy drank it all up before they could get a taste for it.

They found Paddy O'Dell dead one day, sitting on his favorite bar stool, his hand cupped around a bottle of whiskey and a broad smile on his face. It was the way he would have wanted to go, his drinking buddies all agreed. No one asked Mrs. O'Dell what she thought.

The church ladies clucked and cooed over the poor, bereaved family and arranged a splendid wake to send off Paddy O'Dell. Everyone in the neighborhood turned out to say good-bye to the friendly old man they had known for so long. The local bartenders and the owners of the tavern appeared shortly after the funeral parlor doors opened. They were arrayed in deepest mourning, and they looked more bereaved than the widow. Yes, Paddy O'Dell would be sorely missed by some.

The church ladies clustered around the Widow O'Dell and her sons, murmuring condolences and complimenting the family on how natural Paddy looked in his coffin. Frankly, I thought he looked unnatural, seeing as how Mrs. O'Dell refused to have him buried with a whiskey bottle, but I didn't say so aloud, not wanting to be kicked out of the wake.

Apparently, I was not the only one to remark upon the absence of spirits at the wake. Several of Paddy's drinking buddies arrived in a bunch, carrying armloads of Irish whiskey, which they distributed among the guests. Mrs. O'Dell stiffened when she saw them enter the room, but she didn't say a word and pretended to ignore the whiskey glasses being passed around. The sad atmosphere lightened quickly as the mourners topped off their glasses. Several toasts were made in honor of the deceased, and an air of merriment soon prevailed, to the dismay of the Widow O'Dell and the shock of the church ladies.

Old George Tucker was already three-sheets-to-the-wind when he stumbled up to the open casket and made a solemn speech honoring his good friend Paddy. Then he raised his glass in a toast to the deceased and drank it down in one gulp. Behind him, Paddy O'Dell sat bolt upright in his coffin. "What's the matter with me, then George?" the deceased demanded in an irate tone. "I was always good enough to drink with ye in the old days, and now here ye are slighting me at me own wake!"

Everyone in the room gasped. George Tucker turned around and blinked blearily at Paddy. "Sorry, old man," he said. "Have a drink on me!" He poured a slug of whiskey into a glass and handed it to Paddy.

"That's better," Paddy O'Dell said. He drank the whiskey in a long, slow swallow and lay back down in his coffin, the whiskey glass clutched firmly in his hand.

"Now that looks more natural," I said to the local bartender, who nodded solemnly.

Mrs. O'Dell fainted, falling against the massed display of flowers and bringing the whole arrangement crashing to the floor. Her sons had to carry her out, and the church ladies followed, clucking in disbelief, eager to spread the scandalous story far and wide. The funeral director, being a bit of a spoil-

ONE LAST DRINK

sport, shooed the rest of us out the door, and that was the last we saw of old Paddy. Mrs. O'Dell had him buried the next day in a closed casket. She wasn't taking any chances of Paddy coming back again for a repeat performance. Once was enough.

PART TWO
Powers of Darkness and Light

16

The Gold Tooth

ALBANY

Vrouw Stogpens was a stout little woman who lived on a backstreet in the small town of Albany a long time ago, when the Dutch lived in the area. She was a kind lady, though I will confess that she was not too bright. She took in sewing to make ends meet, since her sailor husband had been at sea for the last two years. She always wore two shawls and half a dozen petticoats, so her appearance was that of a short, round ball. Even in the warmest weather, Vrouw Stogpens always complained of the cold.

One rainy evening, Vrouw Stogpens sat huddled next to her fire, trying to justify a quaff of the expensive gin she kept in the corner cupboard. So close to the hearth was she that her knitting nearly fell into the flames when it rolled off her lap. After debating with herself for nearly a quarter of an hour, she reluctantly decided that the more gin she drank now the less she would have later. Promising herself an extra large glass at Christmas, she took her candle and started up the stairs to her bedroom.

A quick, low knock came at her front door. Vrouw

Stogpens stopped climbing the stairs and turned to look down at the door.

"Who is there?" she called fearfully. None of her neighbors would call so late at night.

"Does the wife of Diederik Stogpens live here?" rumbled a gruff male voice from outside the door.

"She does," said Vrouw Stogpens, climbing hastily back down the stairs and setting the candle on a side table.

"Then please let me in, Vrouw Stogpens," said the man.

"Let you in? At this late hour?" said Vrouw Stogpens indignantly. "I do not know your voice, and I despise your manners. Be off with you!"

"I bring news of your husband," the man said through the door.

Vrouw Stogpens hesitated only a moment before going to the door. As I mentioned before, she was none too bright, and it did not occur to her to send the man away until one of her neighbors could come and support her during an interview with a stranger. Besides, it had been two years since she had heard anything from Diederik, and she did want to know what had kept her sailor so long from home. So she opened her door to the stranger.

Into the room breezed a burly, weather-beaten man sporting wild red whiskers and a bold manner. The flame of the candle flickered wildly as he swept into the room, slamming the door shut behind him. He shook the water from his hat, splattering the ceiling and the sand-swept floor, and strolled over to the easy chair next to the fire. He paused only long enough to grab the bottle of gin off the table before settling himself into

the chair with his legs stretched out and his boots among the ashes. He pulled a pipe from his pocket and lit it with a coal from the fire.

Now I am sure that you and I would have recognized him immediately. What with his swashbuckling air and his red whiskers, who else could he be but the infamous privateer turned pirate, Captain Kidd? Onetime resident of New York City, the buccaneer who had captured the fabulously rich Indian ship the *Quedah Merchant,* an all-around scoundrel who had buried more silks, guns, spices, and gold than you and I could imagine, had just made himself at home in the Stogpens' front parlor!

But Vrouw Stogpens led a simple life, and her limited imagination would not stretch far enough to envision a famous buccaneer in her tiny home. It was all she could do to cope with a bold sailor who was smoking a pipe in her clean house and swallowing the last of her gin in a few large gulps.

"Ha!" the captain said, wiping his mouth with the back of his hand. "That is much better." He peered at Vrouw Stogpens, who was glaring at him from beside the door, her hands on her plump hips. "So you're the wid . . . er . . . wife of my friend Dirk Stogpens! A grand fellow, madam, though quite, quite mad!"

"My Diederik, mad?" Vrouw Stogpens fairly quivered with indignation. "He was the steadiest, the most thrifty man that God ever made!"

Captain Kidd looked puzzled for a moment, and then he grinned. The grin displayed a brilliant gold tooth set inside his mouth. "Oh, you mean at home! Of course he was, madam, of course he was at home. But at sea! Well, madam, there weren't no deeper drinker, louder singer, harder swearer, quicker fighter, better card shark, or more swashbuckling wooer of the lad . . . er, hum, that is to say, Dirk was quite a fellow!"

"I am sure you have the wrong man," Vrouw Stogpens said stiffly. "You must be referring to one of the Weekhawk Stogpens."

"No indeed, madam. Dirk gave me his address before he ventured out onto the Grand Banks to overhaul a rich-looking vessel we spotted."

"Overhaul?" asked Vrouw Stogpens, folding her arms across her ample bosom and swelling mightily in fury. "Whatever do you mean?"

"Didn't Dirk tell you he was a privateer?" asked Captain Kidd in amazement, waving the stem of his pipe at her.

"A what?" demanded the good Vrouw.

"A privateer. A pirate."

Vrouw Stogpens's mouth dropped open in shock. She sputtered indignantly for several minutes, finally ordering this terrible stranger out of her house. Captain Kidd just sat in the easy chair watching her with such an air of amusement mingled with sadness that she gradually stopped speaking and they looked at each other in silence.

Slowly, Vrouw Stogpens sat down on a straight-backed chair opposite the captain and nodded her head. "I wondered how he earned so much money while he was at sea," she said. "He didn't bring so much this last time, though, and I have about run out now, what with Dirk being away so long. I've had to take in sewing to keep food on the table. Well, just wait 'til you come home, Dirk Stogpens. I will have some words for you!"

"I'm afraid Dirk won't be coming home, ma'am," Captain Kidd said sadly, his gold tooth glinting in the candlelight. "He met his end while he was overhauling that last brig."

Vrouw Stogpens bowed her head silently, large tears rolling down her cheeks. She had suspected as much when Dirk had stayed away so long from home.

"Still, ma'am, 'twas better to die in a fight than swinging from the end of a rope. That's the fate awaiting me unless you agree to shelter me for your husband's sake," the captain said after a moment of respectful silence.

Vrouw Stogpens looked at the bold buccaneer sitting in her easy chair and finally asked the question she should have asked when he first walked in.

"Just who are you, sir?"

"I am Captain Kidd," he said, rising from the chair and giving her a deep bow.

I am happy to say that Vrouw Stogpens had at least heard of Captain Kidd and knew enough of the terrible deeds associated with the name to be fearful indeed. She fell to her knees, crying, "Spare me, sir! Spare me."

"Now, now," Kidd said in surprise. "I'm not aiming to hurt anyone. There's no pirating to be had in a freshwater town like Albany. And I wouldn't hurt the widow of my good friend, Dirk. See, here's his share of our earnings. I brought it for you, ma'am."

Captain Kidd removed a purse full of coins from his pocket and offered it to Vrouw Stogpens. The sight of all that money

brought her lamentations to a quick end, and after stowing the purse away under her ample garments, she reluctantly agreed to shelter the captain until the search for him was concluded. She showed the captain to the garret and finally made her way to her own chamber to secrete the money under a floorboard before going to sleep.

Vrouw Stogpens was as good as her word. She fed and housed the captain and said nary a word to her neighbors. If she was a bit shocked by his profanity, she was rather thrilled by his tales of adventure. Captain Kidd spent many an evening talking to the widow to ease his boredom, since he dared not venture outside. One night, he told her the story of his gold tooth, which he could put in and take out of his mouth at will. If he tried to smoke his pipe with the tooth in, it would heat up after a few puffs and burn him. After smoking for a while, Kidd took out the tooth, held it up to the light, and said, "Well, ma'am, this gold tooth was given to me by the Devil himself."

"The Devil?" gasped Vrouw Stogpens, shivering and looking thrilled by such horrifying news.

"Indeed, it was the Devil," said Captain Kidd. "He's rather a friend of mine, and he gave me this tooth so I could make gold whenever I wish."

"Gold!" exclaimed Vrouw Stogpens.

Captain Kidd laughed. "Yes, gold. Anything I bite turns to gold. I don't know how long the gift will last, so I spent most of the last month nibbling copper coins, tin cups, and anything else I could find. My shipmates buried the gold on Beeren Island the night before I made my escape from the authorities." The captain paused to take a sip of his whiskey.

"What I am leading up to, ma'am, is that I would be happy to gnaw on some coins or plates for you, by way of paying you for keeping me hidden."

Vrouw Stogpens was delighted. The money under the floorboard would barely last her through the winter, and then there would be no more, since Dirk was dead. She had been spending it prudently, except for a rather extravagant purchase of whiskey to keep Captain Kidd happy. If the captain made some gold for her, she could buy all the things she had dreamed of. Perhaps a new petticoat or two, to keep out the drafts!

Vrouw Stogpens brought the captain all her copper coins and most of her cups and dishes. The captain popped the gold tooth back into his mouth and turned everything into gold. Vrouw Stogpens retired to her bed that night a very happy, and very rich, woman. But as I have said before, and it bears repeating, Vrouw Stogpens was not an intelligent woman. As soon as the shops opened for the day, Vrouw Stogpens was out and about, spending her gold on petticoats and shoes, buckles and fans, lace, girdles, and lots and lots of whiskey. The shopkeepers were all astonished, and soon Vrouw Stogpens was besieged with visitors, agog to know how she had come upon such a fortune.

The sudden influx of company forced Captain Kidd to stay silently in the loft, which made him very grumpy since he could not move about freely or swear loudly, as was his custom. He was also alarmed by all the attention Vrouw Stogpens had aroused and was fearful that the authorities would come and find him hiding out in her house.

THE GOLD TOOTH

After a few days the company dwindled away, and Captain Kidd came back downstairs to spend the evening by the fire. After enjoying a glass of whiskey, the captain took out his pipe and removed the gold tooth in order to smoke in comfort. He had only taken a few puffs when he and Vrouw Stogpens heard the sound of heavy footsteps stomping up the walk. Captain Kidd leaped up in alarm.

"Who could that be?" asked Vrouw Stogpens. A lively rap sounded at the door. As Vrouw Stogpens went to open it, she felt a sudden breeze behind her. She turned in time to see Captain Kidd jumping out the back window and running away in the moonlight. Vrouw Stogpens was astonished. After a moment, she closed the window and went to the door to welcome the members of the church committee, who were petitioning for alms for the poor.

The morning after the abrupt departure of the captain, Vrouw Stogpens woke with an odd feeling in her mouth. When she looked in the glass, she saw the gold tooth wedged in a hollow in her jaw. Vrouw Stogpens was thrilled. Here was reward indeed for having sheltered the captain! She immediately began nibbling on various belongings, turning them all to gold.

Vrouw Stogpens was well on her way to becoming the richest woman in the New World when a sudden thought made her put down the spoon she was preparing to bite. How in the world was she going to eat? She tried to pull the gold tooth out of her mouth, but it was wedged in tightly. She tried biting a crust of bread, but it turned to gold in her mouth. After much maneuvering, she managed to get some soft pieces of bread past the tooth and chewed them with her back teeth.

This was not nearly enough to satisfy her rumbling stomach, but it would have to suffice until she could get the blacksmith to remove the tooth.

Fortifying herself with a nip of whiskey, Vrouw Stogpens went to see the blacksmith. After extracting a large fee from the mysteriously rich Vrouw Stogpens, the blacksmith proceeded to extract the tooth. Clutching the tooth in one hand and her aching jaw in the other, she thanked him and returned home.

Now the blacksmith was very curious about the gold-colored tooth he had removed. It had dented under his turnkey as if it truly were made of gold, and it had left gold streaks on the instrument. He told the story to his wife, who told the neighbor, who told the baker, who informed all his customers, who told their spouses, and soon everyone in Albany was talking about Vrouw Stogpens's mysterious tooth. It did not take the good folk of Albany very long to decide that only a witch would own such a tooth, and soon there were rumors aplenty about Vrouw Stogpens's nocturnal adventures upon a broomstick, and little children ran away when she came walking down the street.

Vrouw Stogpens was very upset by the gossip. One night she took the gold tooth and threw it into the fire. As it burned, it began to give off a high-pitched squealing sound. Suddenly, several blue flames shot up from the surface of the melting gold, each one in the shape of a tiny imp. The imps flew out of the fireplace and surrounded Vrouw Stogpens, pushing her back and forth and laughing as they pulled at her hair and her dress. Each time the imps touched her, Vrouw Stogpens felt colder and colder, until she was chilled to the bone. Finally they disappeared up the chimney, leaving Vrouw Stogpens shivering next to the fireplace as the gold melted into a small puddle that disappeared in a puff of blue smoke.

Vrouw Stogpens wrapped herself in ten petticoats before she went to bed that night, but none of them could warm her. The next morning she was feverish and her chest was heavy with pneumonia. By the time her reluctant neighbors came to her house to see why Vrouw Stogpens had not emerged for more than a week, the widow was beyond the aid of mortal man. She died a month to the day after Captain Kidd escaped out her back window. As for Captain Kidd, well, his pursuers eventually caught up with him, and he was hanged.

17

The Night Riders

COPAKE

I was a small girl when I first saw one of Francis Woolcott's thirteen night riders. My father usually dealt with the night riders when they came each month to collect the levy that the wizard Woolcott imposed upon each of his neighbors in return for leaving them in peace. Father always made Mother and me work inside on the day of the levy, and he insisted that the windows remain shuttered until after the night rider had left the farm. I don't think he wanted the night riders to know anything about his family. But I was a curious child and determined to see what all the fuss was about.

One levy day, when I was four, I looked through a crack in an upstairs shutter and watched my father handing a cloaked figure a side of beef. It looked like a normal business transaction, the kind of thing my father did every day, except there was none of the joking that usually accompanied such a transaction. My father's face was grim and his eyes were full of fear. The cloaked figure of the night rider made me shiver, though it was the height of summer. The night rider was very tall, and a mist obscured the features of his face. He handled the side of beef with ease, though it had weighed down my father, who was not a puny man. The night rider looked up suddenly, gazing right at the window through which I was peeking. I jumped back at once, gasping in fear. When I looked again, the night rider had vanished, and there was no trace of him in the lane.

Stories about Francis Woolcott were rife around our small community. At school, I heard about Farmer Raught's pigs, who had taken to walking upright on their hind legs and trying to talk like men after he cheated the wizard out of his levy. My friend Mary told me that her father once angered the wizard and the very next day his horses had been frozen into immobility halfway through a plowed field. Mary's father had been unable to move them for nearly three hours, no matter how he whipped, tugged, and cursed. After he sent a written apology to the wizard's house, the horses immediately started to move again and finished plowing the field in record time. The tales of Francis Woolcott's exploits were endless! Cows gave blood instead of milk, flocks of blackbirds would fly into a field and ruin a harvest, children would be compelled into doing strange and dangerous things, and the night riders rode enchanted black horses throughout the night, stealing goods and working dark magic at the wizard's bidding.

I saw the wizard only once, as he rode his bay mare past the church one Sunday on his way home. He was a tall, dark man, with a weathered face and a shock of gray hair. I hadn't realized he was so old. He had worn a cruel little smile on his face, as if he were aware of all the attention he was causing,

THE NIGHT RIDERS

and enjoyed it. The congregation was filing out of the church sanctuary as he rode by, and all sound ceased as each person recognized the wizard who plagued all our lives. Even the minister fell silent. I had heard at school that the minister paid a levy to Francis Woolcott in exchange for the souls of his congregation. I didn't know if the rumor was true. We watched until the wizard was out of sight. Only then did people begin to stir and murmur among themselves.

The year I turned fifteen, my father had to travel down to the city on business. That month, he told us grimly, Mother and I would have to pay the night riders ourselves. On levy day, my mother and I lugged a heavy barrel of cider up from the root cellar and rolled it out to the yard. It was nearly noon, but the night rider had not yet arrived. I went toward the lane to watch for the night rider, both eager for and dreading his arrival. When I approached the gate, I saw a funny mist floating next to the hedge that bordered the lane. As I squinted at the misty spot, it hardened into the cloaked figure of a man. At least, I thought it was a man, though I couldn't see his face. The mist that had clouded his form seemed to linger across his features, so I could not make them out.

"You have talent, pretty one," the night rider said softly, so my mother couldn't hear him. "My master likes talent."

I shuddered in fear, but could not help staring at the dark figure standing so close to me that I could have reached out and touched him.

"Come here, Sylvia," my mother called. There was a note of fear in her voice.

I went to stand beside my mother, and we watched in

silence as the night rider lifted the heavy barrel with ease and placed it on his shoulder.

"Francis Woolcott thanks you," the night rider said mockingly. Then he vanished. I couldn't believe my eyes. One moment I was looking into the mist-shrouded face, and the next I was staring at the distant barn.

I could tell my mother was uneasy about my encounter with the night rider. When my father returned, I listened to them discussing the matter long into the night. I wondered what the fuss was all about. I would soon find out.

Around midnight, we were jarred awake by the sound of a huge voice booming inside our house.

"Farmer Daniels! I would speak with you!" The voice echoed and reechoed through my room, shaking the rafters. I leaped out of bed and ran to my parents' room. Father was already up and looking out the window. Seated upon his bay mare, with all thirteen of his night riders behind him, was Francis Woolcott.

"Stay here," my father said to my mother and me. He hurried downstairs and out the front door in his nightshirt, not bothering to dress.

"What do you want, Francis Woolcott?" my father asked angrily, though I could see he was shaking with fear. "This is a hardworking, Christian household. We need our sleep. We have paid your ungodly levy this month. What more do you want from us?"

I stood at the window, watching my father confronting the wizard and his night riders, while my mother knelt beside the bed, praying for his safety.

"My housekeeper perished in an unfortunate accident last week," Francis Woolcott said smoothly, his voice lingering just a bit on the word "unfortunate" in a suggestive manner. "I want your daughter, Sylvia, to take her place. I am told she has talent."

I gasped in fear, remembering the words of the night rider. The wizard looked up at the window where I stood, and our eyes met. My knees were shaking, but I glared fiercely at him, thinking: *You big bully.* He smiled a little, as if he could read my thoughts, and then looked back at my father.

"Never!" my father shouted. "You may take my animals and my crops, but you will never take my daughter."

"Be careful, Master Daniels," Francis Woolcott said softly. "You do not want to make me angry."

Behind him, several of the night riders stirred threateningly and moved their horses forward. But my father was too furious to be frightened by the wizard's minions.

"Do your worst, foul wizard. God will take care of me and my family," Father shouted. He stomped into the house, slamming the door behind him.

Francis Woolcott stared thoughtfully at the front door, and then looked up at me. Our eyes locked again, and this time I was not afraid. I stood proudly, daring him to do his worst. He smiled at me, and I saw that his teeth were crooked. Then he bowed mockingly, wheeled his horse, and rode away. One by one, the night riders followed their master down the lane and out of sight.

Father came into the bedroom, holding a bottle of brandy. He was shaking from head to toe. Mother leaped up from her knees and they clung together, pulling me into their embrace and rocking silently back and forth. We knew, all three of us, what was going to happen.

It started with the cows. In the early morning when I went to milk them, blood-red milk poured forth from their udders. I threw it away. When my father tried to hitch up the wagon, the horses froze in place as if their hooves were nailed to the ground. They were unable to move until my father put the wagon away. Grim-faced, he saddled one of the plow horses and rode to town to visit the minister. The minister prayed over him in secret but refused to publicly defy the wizard. On his way home, my father was thrown from his horse when a strange animal ran out of the woods right in front of him.

At noontime, I found two of our pigs strolling through the front yard, walking upright. They seemed to be discussing the weather in short snorts that sounded like words spoken in a foreign language. At dusk, a fox got into the henhouse and killed all the hens but two that had managed to fly up into a tree.

During the night, rabbits got into our kitchen garden and ate everything. There was no milk again the second morning of our misfortunes. When I went to slop the pigs, I found them sitting upright in a semicircle. It sounded like they were discussing politics in a sophisticated-sounding foreign tongue. I had to restrain myself from inviting them into the house for a cup of tea. Then our dog, Molly, started flinging herself against the side of the barn. Again and again, she would race toward the barn and crash her head against the hard wood, almost knocking herself out each time. We had to tie her up to stop her from killing herself.

During the afternoon, a giant flock of hungry blackbirds descended on the crops. Mother, Father, and I ran through the fields all afternoon shooing them away, trying to save our harvest. The birds departed at dusk and we made our weary way back to the house. As darkness fell, the wind rose, howling and shrieking around our house all night, sounding like the voices of the damned screaming in agony against the tortures of hell. None of us got any sleep.

My mother's sister came for a visit the next morning with her three children. She exclaimed in horror when she heard of our misfortune but could not offer any solutions to our dilemma. I knew then that there was only one way out of all this trouble. I would have to go and work for the wizard.

Suddenly, we heard a shout from the front yard. "Hup! Hup! Hup!" a familiar voice boomed. My three little cousins leaped to their feet like dogs being summoned by their master. Their eyes were glazed, and they pranced out the door and into the yard. We ran after them, and saw them dancing around and around Francis Woolcott's bay mare. The wizard pointed up to the barn roof, and the children ran into the barn. I hurried after them, but they were supernaturally quick, and before I could catch them they were up in the hayloft, out the window, and clambering up the ladder to the roof. My aunt screamed and ran to fetch my father from the field. Grimly, I followed them, refusing to look down as I clambered up the rickety ladder. I caught the littlest girl by the arm and held on tightly, but I could not restrain the others for long.

Down in the yard, Francis Woolcott was laughing.

"Stop!" I shouted down at him. "Stop this at once! They will be killed!"

"I need a housekeeper, Sylvia Daniels," the wizard called up to me. My little cousin jerked out of my grasp and walked to the very edge of the barn roof. She stood teetering back and forth, her eyes glazed. "Will you come with me?"

I put my arms around my small cousin so that if she fell from the barn roof, she would take me with her. The wizard frowned at me and sent my other cousins over to stand on the edge of the roof just out of my reach. My father and my aunt came running into the yard, shouting at the wizard to let us go. Francis Woolcott waved a hand at them, and they were frozen in place like a pair of statues. My mother stood staring back and forth between my father and me in terror. I took a deep breath, clutching my little cousin tightly to my chest.

"I will come," I said.

***

The deal was simple. I would work as an indentured servant for Francis Woolcott until I was twenty-one, and then I would be free to leave his employ. In return for my services, my family would not be required to pay the wizard's levy until such time as I left the wizard's house. Francis Woolcott also promised that I could return to my home for a few hours each month to visit my parents.

We hated the plan, but I would not allow the wizard to continue torturing my family, and my determination overruled my father's objections. I packed my belongings in a satchel, and my father drove me in the wagon to the wizard's house.

The house was large and the gardens were well-groomed.

There was no sign of Francis Woolcott when we arrived. I kissed my father good-bye, clinging to him for a moment as I had not done since I was a tiny child, and then I went to the servant's entrance and knocked on the door. It was opened by one of the night riders, who ushered me in and took me to a small chamber off the kitchen.

"This is your room," he said. I looked at him sharply. His features were blurred, but his voice sounded young and vaguely familiar.

"My master wishes to see you in the study," he added.

I nodded and put my satchel on a chair. Then I followed him to the study, where Francis Woolcott sat behind a massive desk, working on some papers. The wizard dismissed the night rider with a wave of his hand and beckoned me closer. He explained my duties, which included keeping the house clean, cooking the meals for him and for his night riders, and caring for all the livestock save the horses. In exchange, I would be fed, housed, and my parents would be left alone. The night riders would acquire any supplies I needed for the household.

Francis Woolcott explained my duties with an air of care-less indifference, at odds with the intent way he studied me with his eyes. Abruptly, he said, "If you wish, I could also teach you magic for one hour of each day."

I stared at him, shocked. Magic?

"You have talent, child. I do not like to see talent wasted."

For a moment, I was tempted. To wield power such as I had seen the wizard display made my mind reel. But the price, I knew, would be my soul. I shook my head.

"No, Master Woolcott. I will not study magic with you," I said.

To my surprise, the wizard chuckled. "Suit yourself, Mistress Daniels. But if you ever change your mind, you have only to speak up. You are dismissed."

I curtsied and made my way back to the kitchen to unpack my things. When I finished, the young night rider appeared in the kitchen as if by magic. He showed me where the food and supplies were kept and gave me a tour of the house and grounds. I listened carefully to his instructions, trying to remember where I had heard his voice. It was only as he wished me farewell and disappeared out the servants' entrance that I knew him.

My hands shook as I prepared the evening meal and thought about the young night rider. He was Ben Johnston, the oldest son of our neighbors. His parents' farm bordered ours. I had known him, and hero-worshipped him, all my life. Ben was six years older than me, and he had been very patient with the little neighbor girl who followed him around and tried to do everything he did.

When I was eight, Ben was sent to live with relatives, who had offered to send him to an expensive boarding school. At least, that was the story his parents and siblings had told us. We had never questioned the tale, even though that was the first time the Johnstons had mentioned rich relatives. I realized that Frances Woolcott must have threatened the Johnston family as he had mine, and his price was their eldest son. Ben would never have come willingly. Some of the men and boys in town would have liked to serve the wizard, I knew, but not Ben. I wondered how many of the thirteen night riders were prisoners like Ben and me.

The days quickly fell into a pattern. Each morning and at noon, I would serve breakfast and dinner to Woolcott and his night riders. In the evening, the night riders dined alone, and I brought supper on a tray to the wizard's office. Each night before I left his office, Francis Woolcott would ask me if I wished to study magic, and I would say *no*. Every day I cleaned the great house from top to bottom and fed and watered the livestock, though I was not allowed near the horses. Each of the fabulous black horses was cared for by his night rider, and the wizard himself took care of the bay mare. Any time I went near the stables, one of the night riders would drive me away with harsh words, and the wizard would scold me when I brought his supper tray.

In the few minutes of free time I had left after chores, I would read. The wizard had made his library available to me, and I read as many books as I could, hungry for knowledge of the wide world and its workings. I was also trying to discover, if I could, a way to defeat an evil wizard. I think Francis Woolcott knew that was my goal, and it amused him. Sometimes, he would keep me in his study while he ate, and we would discuss the books I had read. Evil he might be, but Francis Woolcott was also intelligent and well-read, and I enjoyed our conversations.

I also came to know the thirteen night riders, many of whom I had known before they were claimed by Francis Woolcott. Four had been farmers, two were sailors, and one had been an attorney before the wizard took them. The other six I did not know, nor did I wish to. They served the wizard because they believed in his evil practices and wanted to share in his power. I was not even sure if they were human or . . . something else.

Francis Woolcott could summon the night riders from anywhere without uttering a word. He would close his eyes as if he were speaking directly into the night riders' minds, and the next moment a night rider would appear out of nowhere to answer his call. It was spooky, the first time I saw him summon a night rider that way. But I soon grew used to it and wondered if I could learn to call them in the same manner. It would be much quieter and more effective than ringing the dinner bell.

The night riders never spoke of their lives before coming to serve the wizard. But Ben had always been able to read me well, and he knew that I knew who he was and why he was there. He did his best to shield me from the attentions of the "bad six," as I had come to call the volunteer night riders in my mind. He would come to talk with me whenever his duties allowed, as if speaking to me gave him comfort. I hope it did.

The night riders roamed far and wide each day, collecting the wizard's levy and doing his errands throughout the town and country. I never left the house and grounds except for the few hours each month when I went to visit my family. I told them nothing about my life at the wizard's house. Instead, we spoke about the farm, the town, and other family matters. Francis Woolcott always ordered one of the night riders to accompany me to my family's house to protect me, he claimed, though I suspect it was to ensure I returned without fuss.

Usually, it was Ben who came with me. He would stand in the corner wearing his massive cloak with his face magically shielded, a dark figure that weighed heavily upon my parents' minds even though they never referred to him. But I took comfort in his presence, knowing that he was drinking in the reminder of his real home, and I led the conversation as often as I could to his family.

I was awakened just after midnight one evening, two months after my arrival, by the quiet sound of many feet walking down the stairs and exiting the house. I threw a dark cloak over my nightclothes and followed the night riders and Francis Woolcott out to the stables, which I saw with astonishment were empty of the proud dark horses the night riders usually rode. Each of the night riders entered the empty stable and came out carrying a bundle of oat straw. They carried their bundles into the center of a grove of ash and chestnut trees and placed them in a circle around the wizard. It was the dark of the moon, and the only light came from the tip of the wizard's staff as he raised it over the bundles of straw, chanting in a language that sounded foul to my ears. Before my eyes the bundles of straw transformed into thirteen dark horses that could run like the wind but could not cross moving water, and fell apart at the stroke of midnight thirty days after their creation. I had read about such creatures in one of the books I had borrowed from the wizard's library. These horses needed neither food nor sleep and could outrun any living creature, since they never wearied of the hunt. Their eyes glowed red in the dark grove, and I huddled behind an ash tree and prayed the wizard would not see me. Francis Woolcott sent his night riders out on an errand that evening, and the demon horses thundered out of the grove just inches away from where I hid. He had spoken too low for me to hear where he was sending them, and I thought it better that I did not know. I did not move from my hiding space for an hour after the wizard made his way back to the mansion. Finally, I crept back to the house and lay sleepless in my small bed until dawn.

Francis Woolcott was the only one who came to breakfast the next morning. His night riders would be away for several days, he explained smoothly. I nodded without speaking and put away the rest of the food I had prepared. For almost a week, only the wizard appeared at the table for meals. I was quite lonely without Ben and the other night riders. I spent much of my time reading and wondering what the night riders were doing so far from home. As the days passed, I began to worry. My supplies were getting low, and if the night riders did not return soon, someone would have to purchase food. Timidly, I broached the topic with the wizard after taking the supper tray to his study.

"If you need any supplies, you will have to go to town by yourself. Perhaps it would be best," he added, "if you drove into the next town to get the supplies. It would help maintain the fiction your parents have created about your absence. Unless you wish the truth to be known?"

I shook my head at once, and the wizard smiled. "I thought not," he said, handing me a bag of coins with which to purchase the supplies I needed.

The next morning I hitched old Jack the donkey to the cart and drove him to the next town. It was a long way, and it was nearly dark when I left town to begin my journey back to the wizard's mansion. I had barely reached the inn just outside of town when the wheel fell off the wagon. I groaned and climbed down, knowing I would need help getting the wheel back on. Just then, two soldiers staggered out the front door of the inn. I saw at once that they were drunk, and neither of them looked trustworthy. I shrank back a little, suddenly afraid, as they spotted my predicament and came toward me.

"Looks like the pretty lady needs some help," one of the soldiers slurred, his eyes undressing me as he approached. I wanted to slap the lustful look off his face, but he was twice my size and weight. His friend came up behind me and grabbed my shoulders. "Give us a kiss, love," he said, pulling me against him. I gave a shriek, which he muffled with his hand. I kicked him in the shins, struggling to free myself. He just laughed at my efforts and started pawing me.

Night riders! Help me! I shouted inside my head, willing them to hear me the way they heard Francis Woolcott. *Ben! I need you!*

The first soldier swore suddenly and grabbed his friend's arm. "Let her go," he gasped. The second soldier dropped me so hard I fell to the ground at his feet. I was breathing heavily, trying not to cry. I wondered why they had stopped mauling me, so I turned over and looked.

Thirteen dark night riders astride thirteen dark horses were in a semicircle behind my donkey cart. They neither spoke nor moved, but the menace they conveyed sent the two soldiers running for their lives. I covered my face with my hands and burst into tears of relief. Ben slid off his horse, picked me up,

and wrapped my cloak over my torn dress. Two of the night riders fixed the wheel on the donkey cart, and one of them drove it home while Ben put me up on his horse and took me back to the wizard's house. He carried me to my little room off the kitchen and laid me on the bed. "Rest," he ordered. "We will take care of everything."

I nodded wearily, the shock of my attack giving way to an overwhelming need for sleep. Just for a moment, before he turned away, the mist that clouded his face lifted, and I saw Ben clearly for the first time since I was eight. Ben's face had lost the boyhood roundness I remembered. He had an angular face now with a determined chin, grim lines around his mouth, and golden-brown eyes that were full of concern for me. I caught my breath, for he was very handsome.

The night riders were all gathered for breakfast the next morning, and I could see each of their faces clearly. Whatever spell prevented folks from seeing their faces no longer affected me. Save for Ben, they were mostly middle-aged men. Some of the faces matched those of men I recollected from early childhood; men who had "gone away" to seek their fortunes. And six of the faces were not human. Their teeth were too sharp, their ears just a bit too pointed, and something about their eyes hinted at sights no mortal had ever beheld.

Each of the night riders, even the "bad six," inspected me anxiously to make sure I was all right. When Francis Woolcott entered the dining room, he looked me over from top to bottom before saying, "Well done my dear. Your talents are even greater than I had come to expect. It is no easy task to call one of my night riders, and you summoned them all." I did not know how to answer him, so I just started dishing up the food.

From that day on, I never used the dinner bell to summon the night riders. I just sent out a mental dinner call and they came. I would no sooner think that the wood box needed filling than one of the night riders would appear with a pile of wood in his arms. When the barn cat I had adopted got stuck in a trap, two of the night riders arrived to help release her and a third splinted her broken leg. The attentions of the other night riders made Ben a little jealous, I think. He started hanging around the kitchen more than ever, and sometimes I would have to shoo him away so I could get some work done. The wizard seemed pleased by his night riders' devotion to me. I felt almost happy at times, when I forgot how I came to be living at the mansion and for whom I was working.

***

I had been working for the wizard for more than a year when I noticed a change in him. Francis Woolcott seemed to age overnight. He breathed heavily after climbing the stairs, he walked with a bit of a stoop, and he often felt cold. He had me build up the fire in his study several times a day to keep out the chill.

I sat back on my heels one evening after making the fire and watched the flames crackle in satisfaction. I always enjoyed a good fire on a cold evening.

"Well, Sylvia, my child, the devil will come for me soon," said Francis Woolcott from his easy chair. He sat with a blanket around his shoulders, a book open on his lap. He looked every one of his ninety years as he put on his spectacles with shaking hands. "Then you will be free to go home. Or to marry young Ben, if he ever gets up enough nerve to ask you," he added with a sly grin.

I blushed and said, "Whatever do you mean?"

The wizard just laughed. "Do you think I have missed the way Ben gets clumsy every time you enter the room? How he lights up when you smile at him? He will make you a fine husband, Sylvia. Neither of you has ever bent to my will. When the devil comes for me and my night riders, he will leave you both alone." He began coughing suddenly, a terrible cough. I leaped to my feet, worried, and hurried to get him a drink.

"Master, you are ill," I said as I put a cup into his hand.

"I am dying at last," Francis Woolcott said, after drinking deeply of the water I had poured for him. "Many of the good folk in this town will thank God for it. You most of all, eh Sylvia?" I did not reply. I hated the wizard, didn't I? To my shame, I could not answer that question. Francis Woolcott was evil and self-centered and a tyrant. But he was also kind and intelligent and a good master. I was confused and hurried away to finish my nightly chores.

Francis Woolcott did not get out of bed the next morning, or for many mornings following. One of the night riders brought the doctor, who confirmed what the wizard told me. Francis Woolcott was dying at last. The preacher refused to visit the dying wizard, which was just as well, for Francis Woolcott cursed me soundly when I suggested the idea. He kept raving that the devil would come for him, and after all I had seen in that house, I thought he was right. Many of the neighbors refused to come and comfort the dying man, as was the custom. But my parents came. It was more out of concern for me than for the wizard, but he welcomed them anyway, though he grimaced at the sight of my father's prayer book and made him put it away.

All the night riders were gathered in the room, as if they sensed that the end was near. Darkness was falling, and with it came a ferocious storm, the likes of which I had never seen. The thunder roared overhead, the wind howled, and the lightning struck again and again just outside the window of the wizard's room, making my skin sizzle. I sent my parents down to the kitchen, suddenly afraid of what might happen to them if the devil really did come for the wizard.

At the height of the storm, Francis Woolcott reared up in his bed, his face taking on a strange, horrible look of recognition. "Master!" he shouted. A flash of purple fire filled the window, and for a moment I thought I saw an evil, pointed face in the flames as the smell of sulfur filled the room. The devil held out a clawed hand toward Francis Woolcott. The room filled with a blinding flash as the wizard touched the devil's hand, and when my eyes cleared, I saw that the wizard was dead, and that six of the thirteen night riders had disappeared, leaving only their dark cloaks behind them. The remaining night riders stood blinking in the candlelight, their faces clearly visible to all for the first time. They smiled at me, and I smiled back. Then they hurried from the room, and I knew they were going home to their families. Ben lingered for a moment in the doorway, and I nodded to him to go ahead without me. My parents and I would bury the wizard.

The night riders had already prepared the grave, and my father buried Francis Woolcott without ceremony and without any prayers. The wizard had asked us to notify his attorney that he was dead, and we did so on the way home. To our astonishment, the roads were dry, and no one in town had heard the terrible storm that had raged at the wizard's house. It had been, my father concluded, the coming of the fiend. Remembering the face I had seen in the purple fire, I did not doubt he was right.

Great was the rejoicing in our town when people learned that Francis Woolcott was dead, and the tariff with him. Great was the astonishment when several families regained loved ones who had decided to "retire" from their travels and make their way back home. Great was my disbelief when the attorney informed me that I was the sole heir of Francis Woolcott, and that all his property and belongings were mine to do with as I wished.

Ben and I discussed the matter and decided we did not want the money or the land. So I sold the house and grounds and disbursed the money among the families from whom the wizard had taken tariff for so many years. Extra was given to the families of the night riders, since the wizard had taken their sons from them. Ben and I kept nothing for ourselves. Our freedom was enough.

Ben and I married and settled on a small plot of land bequeathed to us by both sets of parents. We raised three sons and two daughters, all of them blessedly normal. All my life I retained my ability to mentally call my husband and all the former night riders, and Ben retained his ability to ride any horse like the wind and to appear suddenly wherever he was summoned. In the end we were none the worse for it.

18

Rival Fiddlers

BROOKLYN

It had been a good night for a wedding. The weather was perfect, the bride beautiful, and the schnapps plentiful. Perhaps a tad too plentiful! Joost was distinctly wobbly when at last he started walking home with his pockets full of the money he'd earned playing at the wedding, his fiddle under his arm.

Joost could not remember the last time he had felt so happy. His heart was light, even though his feet didn't seem to be functioning properly and he wasn't quite sure which way was up. Of course, it was the stars' fault. Normally the stars appeared in the sky, but tonight Joost saw stars everywhere he looked.

Joost tripped along the road, weaving back and forth and chanting, "One star here, and one star there. And what is that fence doing in the sky?" Joost peered curiously up at the fence (at least he thought he was looking up) and then decided to sit down (at least he thought it was down) on a rock beside the road to wait for the universe to straighten itself out.

For a while, Joost watched the stars dipping and swaying and rolling around and around.

"Goodness me," he said after a moment, "I believe the stars are trying to dance."

Taking up his fiddle, he struck up a wild jig, improvising the tune to match the rolling, spinning stars all around him. He was playing better than he had ever played before in his life, and the stars seemed to take up the tune and dance along to his fiddle.

And then Joost heard the tolling of a bell. It was midnight. Joost was horrified. He was so caught up in his fiddling that he had broken the Sabbath! Something terrible was sure to happen to him, he knew, and yet he just couldn't stop fiddling. The tune was so lovely, and he was playing so well. Oh well, he had already broken the Sabbath, so he might as well finish the song.

As Joost sawed away at the strings, he became aware of a wild, sweet harmony entwining around his melody. He looked around and saw a tall stranger with a thin face and a pointed, clipped beard fiddling beside him.

Joost paused his song for a moment, and the stranger paused with him. Joost exclaimed, "Where the devil did *you* come from?"

The stranger gave him a wicked smile, but did not answer.

"And how do you know this music?"

"I know this song well, my friend," said the stranger. "It's called 'The Devil's Joy at Sabbath Breaking.' "

"Liar!" shouted Joost. "It is called no such thing! I just created the tune this minute."

"Yet you notice that I followed you flawlessly," said the stranger. Joost considered this. Yes, the stranger had certainly followed his every note as if he knew the tune intimately.

Joost nodded. "You're not too bad at following," he allowed.

"I am even better at leading! Can you play 'Go to the Devil and Shake Yourself'?" asked the stranger.

Joost was offended. "Anyone can play that tune!" he said. "And I will lead, stranger. I play second to none!"

"Well then, you lead. But I bet your soul that I will best you at any song you play."

"Done!" said Joost, rising rather unsteadily to stand on the rock and putting his fiddle under his chin.

Joost started fiddling "Go to the Devil and Shake Yourself" and the stranger matched him note for note. Joost kept playing, switching from song to song, playing anything and everything he had ever learned. The stranger matched him air for air, easily proving his mastery over the fiddle. But Joost was inspired that night, and his music danced and sang and seemed as if it would pull the soul right out of the world. Not even the stranger's expertise could match him.

As dawn approached, Joost sounded the first notes of a famous old Dutch hymn calling all pious men to prayer. At the sound of the hymn, the stranger swore and broke off his fiddling. His eyes flashed red and sparks shot off his body, blinding Joost.

"You've beaten the devil," the stranger cried angrily, stamping his foot on the rock. He disappeared with a flash of fire. The explosion threw Joost 20 feet out into the field, and he was knocked senseless for several hours.

Joost was roused by a herdsman pouring a jug of water over him.

RIVAL FIDDLERS

"Had one too many schnapps, Joost?" the herdsman asked cheerfully. "I heard the wedding feast was grand."

Joost sat up, clutching his head. "Grand indeed," he agreed. "Have you seen my fiddle?"

"Right here she be," said the herdsman, handing it to him. Joost thanked the man and staggered to his feet, his head pounding. He made his way back to the road, wondering if he had dreamed the fiddle contest against the devil. When he reached the rock on which he had sat fiddling the night before, he stopped and stared in astonishment. At the very center of the rock was a single hoofmark where the devil had stamped his foot in rage when he lost the fiddling contest.

Joost gave a yelp of alarm when he saw the devil's mark on the stone. For the first time, he realized just how close he had come to losing his soul. Clutching his fiddle to his chest, Joost ran all the way home. He never fiddled on the Sabbath again.

19

Baker's Dozen

ALBANY

So, my grandson, you want to hear a story about the old days, eh? Would you like to hear the tale of how your grandfather met Sinterklaas (Saint Nicholas), who is the patron saint of merchants, sailors, and children? Very well then, I will tell you!

Back in the old days, I had a successful bakeshop in Albany. My only rivals were the knikkerbakkers—they were the bakers of marbles—and they could not hold a candle to me. I had a good business, a plump wife—your grandmother—and a big family. I, Volckert Jan Pietersen Van Amsterdam, was a happy man.

But for all my good fortune, I was a little spooked by the stories I had heard of witches and their evil craft. 'Twas my greatest fear in those days, the fear of being bewitched. I was a good, law-abiding man who went to church each Sunday with my family, but I could not shake my fear of witches. I think now that this was caused by my lack of trust in Saint Nicholas to look after me and my family properly. And perhaps I was unconsciously aware that my stingy nature in my dealings with my fellow man might someday cause me a problem.

Trouble did come to my door the last day in December of 1654. I had spent the whole month making New Year's cakes, gingerbread, mince pies, and *speculaas*—molded spice cookies of Saint Nicholas. It was these cookies that started my troubles the day before the New Year began.

It had been a very busy day in my shop. I was relaxing behind the counter and having a second glass of spirits to celebrate my gains when a sharp rap came at the door and an ugly old woman whom I had never seen before entered my shop.

"I wish to have a dozen New Year's cookies," cried she, pointing to my Saint Nicholas cookies that were sitting out on a tray.

"My good Vrouw, you do not need to shout so loudly. I am not deaf," I chided her as I counted out twelve cookies.

The old Vrouw's eyes narrowed when she saw the cookies. "Only twelve?" she asked.

I knew at once what she wanted. I was an educated man. I had heard about the bakers in England who gave thirteen loaves to their customers rather than a round dozen. Back in the thirteenth century, the English had imposed strict regulations upon their bakers regarding the weight of a loaf of bread. However, my grandson, it was impossible to ensure that every loaf of bread would meet the regulation weight, as any good baker could have told you. In those days, it became the custom for English bakers to add an extra loaf to their dozen to guarantee that they made the weight for their order. This was a long time ago, but some English bakers still abided by this custom.

I did not know how this ugly, uneducated old woman had heard about the English baker's dozen, but somehow she knew the custom and wanted me, a Dutchman, to abide by it. I was appalled! Without paying for extra, she wanted more?

"I asked for a dozen cookies, and you only give me twelve," the woman said.

"A dozen *is* twelve, my good Vrouw, and that is what I have given you. That is what you ordered and that is what you pay for."

"I want another. I ordered a dozen cookies, not twelve," said the old woman.

I tell you, my grandson, I was upset. I was an honest man. I always gave my customers exactly what they paid for. But I was also a thrifty man. To give away something for nothing? This was against my nature.

"Do I look like an Englishman?" I shouted. "I have a family to support. If I give away all my cookies, how can I feed my family? A dozen is twelve, Vrouw, not thirteen! If you want another cookie, you can go to the devil to get it!"

My grandson, this was a foolish thing for me to do. I, who was so afraid of being bewitched, had just shouted at an ugly old woman of whom I knew nothing.

"Very well," said she, and left the shop without taking the cookies.

Was I afraid? Not then. I was a fool, and so I raged to myself as I closed the bakeshop and stomped home to tell my wife about the crazy old Vrouw who wanted something for nothing.

That was the beginning of my bad luck. The next day, my cakes were stolen out of my shop and the thieves were never found. Then my bread refused to rise. For a week, every loaf of bread I made was so heavy that it fell right through the oven and into the fire. The next week, the bread rose so high that it actually floated up the chimney. I was frightened when I saw the loaves floating away across the rooftops. That was the first moment I believe myself bewitched. I remembered the old woman then and wondered if she was a witch.

I was upset that a witch would put a spell on me just because of a single cookie. The next week, when the old Vrouw appeared in my shop, demanding a baker's dozen of the latest batch of my cookies, I cursed her soundly and sent her back to the devil from which she came. The old witch left my shop, and I slammed the door behind her.

Things became worse for me. My bread soured and my *olykoeks* (donuts) were a disgrace. Every cake I made collapsed as soon as it came out of the oven, and my gingerbread children and my cookies lost their flavor. Word was getting around that my bakeshop was no good, and one by one, my customers were falling away. I was angry now, and stubborn. I was a God-fearing, churchgoing man, and no witch was going to defeat me. When she came to my bakeshop a third, and then a fourth time to demand a baker's dozen of Saint Nicholas cookies, I told her to go to the devil, and the last time I locked the door behind her.

After that day, my bakeshop was haunted by invisible spirits. While I was baking, invisible hands would take bricks from the oven and throw them at me until I turned black and blue. Each time my wife visited the shop, she was struck with deafness that would last for hours. Rents and tears would appear in my children's clothing, and no matter how often my wife

BAKER'S DOZEN

toiled to mend them, they would reappear within moments.

My customers began to avoid my cursed shop, even those who had come to me every day for years. Everything I baked was either burnt or soggy, too light or too heavy. Finally, my family and I were the only ones eating my baking, and my money was running out. I was desperate. I took myself to church and began to pray to Saint Nicholas, the patron saint of merchants, to lift the witch's curse from myself and my family.

"Come and advise me, Saint Nicholas, for my family is in dire straits and I need good counsel against this evil witch who stands against us," I prayed. Then I trudged wearily back to my empty shop, wondering what to do.

I stirred up a batch of Saint Nicholas cookies and put them into the oven to bake, wondering how this lot would turn out. Too much cinnamon? Too little? Burnt? Underdone? To my surprise, they came out perfectly. I frosted them carefully and put my first successful baking in weeks onto a tray where they could be seen through the window. When I looked up, Sinterklaas was standing in front of me.

I knew him at once, this patron saint of merchants, sailors, and children. He was not carrying his gold staff or wearing the red bishop's robes and mitered hat that appeared on the figure I had just frosted on my cookies. But the white beard and the kindly eyes were the same. I was trembling so much my legs would not hold me, so I sat down on a stool and looked up at the saint standing so near I could have touched him. His eyes regarded me with such sadness it made me want to weep.

"Volckert Jan Pietersen," Saint Nicholas said softly, "I spent my whole life giving money to those in need, helping the sick and suffering, and caring for little children, just as our Lord taught us. God, in his mercy, has been generous to us, and we should be generous to those around us."

I could not bear to look into his eyes, so I buried my face in my hands.

"Is an extra cookie such a terrible price to pay for the generosity God has shown to us?" he asked gently, touching my head with his hand.

Then he was gone. A moment later, I heard the shop door open and footsteps approached the counter. I knew before I looked up that the ugly old woman had returned to asked me for a dozen Saint Nicholas cookies. I got up slowly, counted out thirteen cookies, and gave them to the old woman, free of charge.

She nodded her head briskly. "The spell is broken," she said. "From this time onward, a dozen is thirteen."

She pointed to the tray of Saint Nicholas cookies and said, "I ask you, Volckert Jan Pietersen Van Amsterdam, to swear by the saint that you will be more liberal in the future."

I swore readily, remembering the saint's words to me moments before. And from that day to this, my grandson, I have given generously of my baking, and of my money, and thirteen will always be, for me, a baker's dozen.

20

The Wizard in the Hollow

SAG HARBOR, LONG ISLAND

The wizard had no friends save his three demon familiars, who took the form of black ravens. His tribe was frightened by him, and though he had their respect, there were none who loved him. He had embraced the dark for so long that none with a pure heart would come near him. So he lived alone on Block Island for many a weary year. He grew bitter in his solitude. Perhaps, he reasoned, if he struck a mighty victory against the great enemy of his people, the Montauk chief Wyandanch, he would find the acceptance he craved.

So a time came when Wyandanch and several of his warriors went in secret to Block Island, the territory of the wizard's tribe, seeking eagle plumes to use in their sacred ceremonies. The wizard learned of the chief's presence on the island and alerted his people. The bloodshed that followed was horrendous; in the end, the only survivors were the chief and the wizard.

When Wyandanch returned to his home on Long Island, the wizard secretly followed. The wizard was enraged by the slaughter of his people and was determined to enlist the dark forces to unite against the Montauk chief. There were giants who lived near Napeague, and the wizard petitioned them to unite against Wyandanch. But the giants refused him, so he turned to the renegades, the bitter, and the scorned and sought their support. To no avail.

Even in this new land, the wizard was alone, save for his raven familiars. Enraged and bitter, the wizard determined to do alone what none else would dare. He would topple the chief himself. Hidden within a dark hollow, the wizard worked evil spell after evil spell, each aimed at the mighty Wyandanch. With each new sorcery the wizard's malice grew, and with it his power. It was not long before the great chief of the Montauk began to falter under the weight of the evil spells being pressed upon him. Wyandanch began to lose his prowess in the hunt, and his wise voice was no longer heard within the council.

The Montauk became alarmed at this sudden change in their chief. They knew something was wrong, and the wisest members of their tribe began to search for the cause. In the end, it was one of the renegades who told the tribe about the wizard who hated Wyandanch and had followed him from Block Island, determined to destroy him.

The young men of the tribe were enraged by this attack on their chief. They began searching for the wizard, determined to find him. They interviewed all the outcasts, and one young warrior went to speak to the giants, seeking the hiding place of the wizard.

The giants had been watching the wizard from afar, tracking his movements but not interfering with him as long as he left them alone. But they were open to bribery, and for a price, they told the Montauk where to find him.

The warriors made their plans carefully. In the darkest part of the night, they surrounded the hollow where the wizard

THE WIZARD IN THE HOLLOW

lived and crept stealthily toward his hiding place. The wizard's familiars sensed the approach of the warriors. They leaped skyward, shouting the alarm as they transformed into brilliant creatures of light and shadow and fled out over the ocean. Below them the wizard rose from his hiding place, lifted his arms, and shouted a mighty curse upon the men who sought his death. He called upon his raven familiars to rend the bodies and spirits of the Montauk warriors. But the brave spirits and pure hearts of the young men repelled the raven familiars, and they turned against their master instead. A dense cloud of light and shadow rose from the sea and swept onto the land. The cloud swirled around and around the wizard, obscuring him from the gaze of the watching Montauk warriors. Where the cloud touched the wizard, it burst into flames. The flames flared brighter and brighter against the dark night. Trapped inside the cloud, the wizard shouted his most potent spells, beating at the flames and trying to break free. But the flaming cloud twisted around and around him, pushing him steadily toward the ocean.

The warriors stood in silence, watching as the wizard was swept up into the cloud of flame and carried out to sea. The wizard uttered one terrible, shrieking cry that echoed and reechoed through the night. Then he was gone. With his death, the curse on the chief was lifted, and Wyandanch was whole once more.

Each winter from then until now, the shade of the wizard returns to the hollow from whence he worked his evil spells on the Montauk chief. On dark nights, he can still be heard shrieking his curses through the crisp, cold air.

21

Henry Hudson and the Kaatskill Gnomes

CATSKILL MOUNTAINS

Well now, the great British explorer Henry Hudson spent much of his life searching for the fabled northern passage to the Orient. His first two voyages saw him scurrying all over creation, looking for something that didn't exist and making his crews mighty unhappy.

Hudson's first voyage, in 1607, was for the Muscovy Company. He was captain of the *Hopewell,* and his commission was to find a sea route to the Orient by traveling across the North Pole. You see in those days, several prominent geographers believed the North Pole region grew milder and warmer thanks to five months of constant sunshine. They theorized that by sailing north, the ship would be able to navigate straight across the pole to the Orient through clear waters and open seas. Unfortunately for the geographer's theories, it didn't work! The Arctic remained full of ice and snow, in spite of the constant sunshine, and Hudson finally had to turn the ship around and sail home.

Well, those stubborn Englishmen had to have another go at it. Eight months later, the Muscovy Company sent Hudson and a crew of fifteen out on the *Hopewell* to search for a northeast passage to the East Indies through the Arctic waters north of Russia. As before, Hudson couldn't get the *Hopewell* through the ice-laden waters just past the islands of Novaya Zemlya, so he turned the ship around. Hudson wanted to look for a northwest passage to the Orient, but the crew threatened to mutiny if they did not return home, so home they went.

After this second failure, the English lost interest in finding a northern passage to the Orient. But not good ol' Henry Hudson. No, Hudson still wanted to find the mythical northern passage to the Orient. He thought that the answer might lie in the northwest rather than the northeast. So Hudson went to the Dutch and the French, looking for sponsors. Finally the Dutch East India Company—England's greatest trading rival—hired Hudson to seek a northeast passage to the Orient, unconvinced by Hudon's theory that success lay in a northwestern route.

Hudson set sail on the *Half Moon* with a crew of twenty, heading northeast. It was a cold, stormy journey and his crew got mighty tired of traveling in the icy Arctic waters, so they threatened to mutiny. To calm everyone down, Henry Hudson canceled the northeastern part of his voyage and sailed south, heading toward the east coast of the New World, although if the truth be known, he was fulfilling his own private agenda, searching for a northern pathway to the Orient through western waters. That is how, on September 3, 1609, Henry Hudson sailed the *Half Moon* into the mouth of the great river that later bore his name.

Henry and his crew traded with the American natives living along the river and received some "Turkish wheat"—corn—and tobacco from the people. But not all the natives who met Hudson and his crew were friendly. The crew had some pretty nasty run-ins with some of the natives along the river. Early in the month, five crewmen went north to sound the East River and were attacked. One man took an arrow to the throat and died. After a few more cautious encounters with the natives, Hudson ordered the crew to set sail up the great river. And so it came to pass that on a mid-September day in 1609, Hudson sailed through the narrows and anchored in New York Bay, off the northern tip of Manhattan. On September 14 Hudson reached the widening of the river at Tappan Zee. For a few hours he thought he had at last succeeded in finding the northwest passage to the Orient. However, it became clear by the time he reached the area that would become present-day Albany, that he was mistaken. Hudson sailed 150 miles up-river before reluctantly turning back.

One evening on the return journey, Hudson anchored the *Half Moon* in the shadow of the Kaatskill Mountains. As day darkened into night, Hudson heard the sound of music floating across the mountains and down to the river. Taking a few members of his crew, he went ashore and followed the sound up and up into the Kaatskills. The sound of the music grew louder as Hudson and his men marched through a hollow and up to the edge of a precipice. To their astonishment, a group of pygmies with long, bushy beards and eyes like pigs were dancing and singing and capering about in the firelight.

Hudson realized at once that these were the metal-working

HENRY HUDSON AND THE KAATSKILL GNOMES

gnomes of whom the natives had spoken. One of the bushy-bearded chaps spotted the explorer and his men and welcomed them with a cheer, which his fellows took up at once. The short men surrounded the crew and drew them into the fire-light and the dance. Hudson and his men were delighted with these strange, small creatures, and doubly so once they tasted the hard liquor that these gnomes had brewed. Long into the night the men drank and played ninepins with the gnomes, while Henry Hudson sipped at a single glass of spirits and spoke with the chief of the gnomes about many deep and mysterious things.

Realizing at last how late it was, Hudson looked around for his men. At first, he couldn't locate them. All he saw were large groups of gnomes, laughing and joking as they sprawled around the fire. Then, to his astonishment, he recognized several of the gnomes as his crewmen! They had undergone a transformation. Their heads had swollen to twice their normal size, their eyes were small and piglike, and their bodies had shortened until they were only a little taller than the gnomes themselves.

Hudson was alarmed and asked the chief of the gnomes for an explanation. It was, the chief explained to Hudson, the effect of the magical hard liquor the gnomes brewed. It would wear off when the liquor did. Hudson wasn't sure that he believed the little man. Afraid of what else might happen to him and his crewmen if they continued to linger in such company, Hudson hurriedly took his leave of the gnomes and hustled his severely drunken crew back to the *Half Moon*. The entire group of them slept late into the morning, as if they were under the influence of a sleeping draught. When they awakened, the crewmen who had accompanied Hudson up into the Kaatskill Mountains, aside from ferocious headaches, were back to normal.

Hudson continued on his way down the great river and by October 4, the *Half Moon* had reached the mouth and Hudson and his crew sailed for home. After landing in England, Hudson was arrested for sailing for a rival country to the "detriment" of his own, and he and the English members of his crew never returned to Amsterdam.

In 1610, backed by Sir Thomas Smythe—governor and treasurer of the Virginia Company—Hudson sailed the *Discovery* northwest, looking for a passage to the Orient with a crew of twenty men and two boys. The voyage was plagued with trouble right from the start. Hudson sailed *Discovery* through the stormy, treacherous Arctic waters north of Quebec and into the modern-day Hudson Bay. By November, *Discovery* and her crew were iced into the bay for the winter.

During the winter, one crewman died of exposure, and many others suffered from scurvy or lack of food. It was not until late the next spring that the ship sailed again. After being caught in the ice several more times, the crew despaired of getting home with Hudson as captain. They were nearly out of food, and Hudson seemed to want to continue sailing northwest looking for his fabled passageway. The crew mutinied, and Henry Hudson and eight of his crewmen—one of them his son, John—were set adrift in the Hudson Bay. They were never seen again.

In September 1629, twenty years to the day that Hudson

and his crew met the Kaatskill gnomes, a bright fire appeared on the precipice above the hollow and lively music could be heard floating through the mountains. The Kaatskill gnomes danced and caroused and drank their magic liquor. At midnight, they were joined by the spirits of Henry Hudson and his crew. Merry was their meeting, and the gnomes and the spirits played ninepins all night long. Each time they rolled the ball, a peal of thunder would shake the mountains and the fire would flare up in bolts like lightning. The party lasted until daybreak, at which hour the spirits departed from the hills, with promises to return once every twenty years to drink and play ninepins with the Kaatskill gnomes.

The spirits of Henry Hudson and his crew kept their word. Every twenty years they returned to the mountains to play ninepins with the gnomes and to look out over the country they had first explored together on the *Half Moon*. Now and then, one of the Dutch settlers living in the region came across the spirits as they played ninepins and brought news of the ghosts to a new generation.

A rumor eventually spread among the settlers, claiming that any man foolish enough to drink of the spirits' magic liquor would sleep from the moment the spirits departed the mountain to the day they returned, twenty years later. Most folks discounted the story, although several members of the Van Winkle family swore it was true. Today, true or false, wise folks who walk among the Kaatskills in September do not accept a drink of liquor when it is offered to them. Just in case.

22

The Maid of the Mist

NIAGARA FALLS

I never considered myself a coward. I always faced whatever dangers life threw at me with a brave heart and steady hands. But now my hands were shaking as they gripped the paddle. My canoe was caught in the current and there was no turning back, even if I wished it. And I did not wish it, for life was very bitter to me and I desired a swift end to my anguish. I had buried my husband before his time, and all that was left within me was a terrible pain that could not be healed. After many days of mourning, I realized I could not go on and decided that death would be better than agony.

But when I heard the distant roaring of the great falls, my hands began to tremble, and the peace I had felt when I first set foot in my canoe fled. It was, I think, the realization that there would be physical pain before death that made me shiver and shake. I prayed to the Thunderer that my death would be swift and that my courage would remain with me until the end. Then I threw my useless paddle away as the canoe entered the rapids and I watched the falls growing nearer, the sky reaching down to touch the very edge of the water as it plunged into the abyss. I gripped the sides of the canoe as the current heaved the small craft to and fro, moving me swiftly to my end. I sang softly to myself, a death song that I had been composing for many days. There was no one to hear me, even if I could sing loud enough to pierce through the thunder of the falls, but that was no matter.

The turmoil of the water under my canoe increased, but it did not hide the thunder of the cataract. I could feel droplets, and soon enough I would see the clouds of mist boiling upward from the abyss. Those clouds would screen my final seconds, and for that I was thankful. My canoe reached the brink and seemed to hang for an eternal moment at the edge of the chasm. I leaped to my feet with a cry, determined to show bravery at the end in spite of my trembling. And then I was falling, falling through the clouds of mist.

I had expected pain and swift death. Instead, I was caught and held in a pair of strong arms. I looked up through the swirling mist into the face of my rescuer. In his face I saw the wisdom of the ancients, and his eyes, though fierce, were also kind. He did not speak, but his voice was all around me, in the roar of the cataract above which we were floating. He was Heno, the Thunderer. He had heard my prayer, and instead of giving me courage to die, he was giving me a second chance at life. We floated to the great curtain of water, and he shielded me with his body as he stepped through it into the cavern behind the falls. He placed me on a stone bench in the dim twilight behind the falls, and for the first time since I had buried my husband, I broke down and wept out my anguish at his passing and my relief at my rescue.

THE MAID OF THE MIST

Heno spoke to me then, and his voice was kind. He told me I could live here with him and his family as long as I wished, until my pain had healed. I thanked him, and he showed me to a room where I could change into dry clothing and rest.

I met his sons when I awoke from the first healing sleep I had had since my husband's death. Even through the anguish I felt at my loss, my heart recognized that the Thunderer's younger son mattered to me in a way that no one else—not even my late husband—had ever mattered. I did not speak of my feelings to him at that time, or in the slow, healing days and weeks that followed. But somehow he sensed when my heart had healed enough, and he came to me at that time with soft words of friendship, which swiftly grew into the flames of love.

Heno was pleased by the match, and even better pleased with our son, whom he trained in the ways of the Thunderer. I was as happy now as I had once been sad, and the only thing I missed from my old life was knowledge of my people. Heno sensed my longing, and he would sometimes check on my village and tell me all he had heard and seen of my people. And so many seasons passed in peace and prosperity.

Then one day, Heno appeared in the cavern where I was working. I saw at once that the Thunderer, my husband's father, was troubled. When I asked him what was wrong, the Thunderer told me that a great snake had poisoned the waters of my people, and soon it would return to devour the dead until my people were all gone. I was horrified and asked him what I could do to avert this tragedy. Heno told me that I should go back—just for an hour—and warn my people of the danger. I consented at once, and the Thunderer lifted me through the mighty curtain of water and up, over the falls to the gathering place of my people.

For a few moments, I stood once more among my people, eagerly seeking out familiar faces as I gave them warning about the evil snake that was causing such pestilence among them. I advised them to move to a higher country until the danger had passed, and they agreed. Then Heno came and lifted me up into his arms and took me home.

It was but a few days later that the giant serpent returned to my village, seeking the bodies of those who had died from the poison it had spread. When the snake realized that the people had deserted the village, it hissed in rage and turned upstream, intent on pursuit. But Heno had heard the voice of the serpent. He rose up through the mist of the falls and threw a great thunderbolt at the creature, killing it in one mighty blast. The giant body of the creature floated downstream and lodged just above the cataract, creating a large semicircle that deflected huge amounts of water into the falls at the place just above our home. Horrified by this disastrous turn of events, Heno swept in through the falls and did his best to stop the massive influx of water, but it was too late.

Seeing that our home would soon be destroyed, the Thunderer called for me and his sons to come away with him. My husband caught me and our child up in his embrace and followed Heno through the water of the falls and up into the sky, where the Thunderer made us a new home. From this place, we watch over the people of the earth, while Heno thunders in the clouds as he once thundered in the vapors of the great falls. And still to this day, an echo of the Thunderer's voice can be heard at Niagara Falls.

23

The Hermit's House

ADIRONDACK MOUNTAINS

She was nervous, and she did not know why. It was a perfect place for them to stay for the season; an old, abandoned house where a hermit once lived. Perhaps she was spooked at the idea of sharing the house with a corpse, for the body of the hermit lay enshrined in a birch-bark coffin in the loft. It was an old custom and one no longer popular among the Iroquois people, for which she was thankful. But the hermit had a reputation for being odd, and when he insisted on staying in his home after his death, the folks from the nearby village had done as he wished.

The house was open to any who wanted to stay there, and hunters sometimes spent the night. But the Iroquois women in the nearby village had warned her against stopping there with her baby daughter. The house had a strange reputation, and the hermit himself had told the women of the village to stay away.

She told her young husband what the village women had said, but he only laughed at the gossip. There was good hunting here, her man had declared, and soon they would prosper and he could build a better home for her and their baby daughter. So they traveled along the footpaths until they came to the hermit's house, and they unpacked their few belongings in the front room. She would not, she told her husband, go up into the loft where the hermit's body lay in its birch-bark coffin. Her husband teased her for being cowardly, but she would not be moved from her decision.

Her husband left the house soon afterwards to hunt. She immediately put her daughter in the sling on her back and went to look for roots and berries. It would make a nice addition to whatever her husband killed for supper, she reasoned, although her real purpose was to get out of the hermit's house. She stayed away until her husband returned with the meat, and then went inside to prepare the evening meal for them. Her husband yawned and stretched, tired from his hunting, and climbed up into the loft to rest.

The hut soon filled with the delicious smell of roasting meat. She was sorting through the berries when she heard a muffled cry and the very final-sounding crunch of breaking bones. She stiffened in shock and was about to call out, but some instinct stopped her. As she stared upward, frozen in horror, blood started to drip from the rafters above the place her husband had lain down to sleep. She heard sounds of gnawing and slurping coming from the loft overhead.

On the pretext of getting something from one of the packs, she crept silently to the far corner of the room where she could see up into the loft. A skeleton with glowing red eye sockets was sitting on the legs of her dead husband. Its teeth and chin were covered with blood, as if it had been feasting on his body.

THE HERMIT'S HOUSE

She crept back out of view before the skeleton saw her and was quietly sick in the corner. Her daughter stirred restlessly at her back, and she knew that she had to get away immediately or she and her child would be killed, too.

"I am going to run down to the stream to fetch water for the broth," she called toward the loft. "I will be right back." She took the pail and walked carelessly toward the stream, trying to appear normal. As soon as she was out of sight among the trees, she started to run as fast as she could, back along the footpaths to the nearest village. The baby bounced and bumped in the sling. Not liking the jarring movements, her infant daughter began to cry. Her wails were answered by a terrible howl from the direction of the house. The evil creature had just realized that they were escaping.

The young mother ran as fast as she could through the darkening woods. She could hear the creature's howls growing closer as it pursued them, and she increased her speed, tearing off one of her scarves and throwing it down for the skeleton to maul. She heard the trees rustling behind her, and then the sounds of pursuit stopped for a moment as the beast pounced on her scarf and tore it to bits in its fury. She kept running, her little daughter wailing desperately as she sensed her mother's fear.

Each time she heard the creature drawing close to her, the young mother threw off another scarf for it to savage, until she had none left. Then she threw off her moccasins, one after the other to buy them more time. She was sobbing exhaustedly and was nearly without hope. Her infant was clinging to her hair, too scared even to cry as they fled through the darkness.

She could hear the monster gaining on her, and she had nothing left to shed save the few items keeping her decent enough to enter the village.

The creature's howls were very close now, and she knew that she was unable to run much further. She could see the lights from the Iroquois village through the trees in front of her, though it was still far off. In a last act of despair, she shouted the Iroquois distress cry, hoping someone would be near enough to hear it. To her joy, her call was taken up by women's voices from just outside the wall of the village and answered by the warriors from within. The creature was so close now she could hear it breathing, and she summoned the last of her strength and sprinted to the trees at the edge of the village. Here, her strength failed her, and she collapsed to the ground, her little daughter wailing in terror.

Before the monster could pounce on them, a party of warriors burst through the gates of the village. The creature leaped back into the trees as the warriors surrounded her, searching left and right for her attacker. They swung their torches wide when they glimpsed a figure in the trees, and the skeleton retreated farther into the woods. The young mother lay gasping and sobbing on the ground, too spent to speak. Realizing that it had lost its prey, the creature called to the young mother, "Today the luck was yours. We will see what tomorrow brings."

Then it was gone. The warriors carried the young mother into the village. The women came to tend to her and her child, while the warriors stood guard over them throughout the night. The next morning the woman told the chief her story, and the warriors went immediately to the hermit's house to search for the creature that had tried to kill her. They found her husband dead in the loft of the house, his neck broken and a gaping hole in his side. In the birch-bark coffin, the mouth of the hermit's skeleton was covered with the young man's blood.

Enraged at this act of vampirism, the warriors set fire to the cabin. As the flames encompassed the house, a terrible howling and roaring came from the loft. Warriors were posted at each exit, but a long, low figure leaped through the flames and jumped out the back window. It looked like a jack rabbit, but its howls were not human. It dodged the war clubs thrown at it and escaped between the legs of two warriors. The creature disappeared into the woods, and though the warriors pursued, they did not catch it. But the vampire had lost its human shape and its powers; it did not come again to plague the young woman or her daughter.

24

The Loup-Garou's Debt

MOOERS

Mon Dieu! There is no more stubborn man on earth than your grandpère! *He* says he has a strong will. I tell you, *ma petite,* that he is just plain stubborn and always has been, which is how he came to have trouble with a loup-garou.

Now the loup-garou are men just like anybody else, until they get themselves into some kind of mischief, which makes them susceptible to the workings of the devil. Once the devil has gotten them in his clutches, he transforms them into wolves and makes them do his work. Mostly this happens to those misguided souls who neglect their duties at Easter and Christmas and do not help the poor. But sometimes a man will become a loup-garou because he dies without having settled his outstanding debts, and this bars him from heaven until the creditor forgives the debt before God.

Now it happened many years ago that Henry, an old friend of ours, died while still owing your grandpère two dollars. This may not seem such a large debt to you children, but back in those days, two dollars could pay for several meals. Your grandpère was quite angry with our friend. He swore an oath, saying he would not forgive old Henry his debt even though it meant that Henry's soul would never get into heaven. I chided your grandpère for his unchristian sentiment, but he was stubborn and refused to forgive the debt.

"*Mais non*," he shouted at me. "I will not forgive this debt, not even if Henry himself should come back from the grave and beg for my charity."

These were foolish words, and so I told your grandpère. But once his mind was made up he would no more give in to me than he would to any man or woman. As I said before, he is the most stubborn man *le bon Dieu* ever created.

I think your grandpère was hoping that Henry's ghost would appear to him, so he could refuse to forgive his debt. He stayed awake night after night, peering out the window or sitting grimly by the fire until sunrise. But Henry did not materialize, which made your grandpère very cranky indeed.

One winter night, your grandpère was out late buying supplies. He hitched our horse to the sleigh right about sunset and started for home through the woods. The moon was full, and it gleamed brightly off the snow as Grandpère drove home. Grandpère noticed a shadow slipping in and out of the trees, following the sleigh. When it glided through a patch of moonlight, he saw it was a large wolf. The wolf's eyes glowed with an uncanny light that made your grandpère's skin crawl with fear. Its feet barely touched the ground as it raced through the deep snow.

Grandpére grabbed his whip and urged the horse into a gallop. The horse was terrified by the large, stealthy creature that was following them and gladly ran when bidden. The

THE LOUP-GAROU'S DEBT

strange wolf easily kept up with the speeding sleigh. Fearing that he would founder his horse if he kept up such a terrible pace in such cold weather, Grandpère slowed the trembling horse to a walk, watching the wolf as he did so. Immediately, the wolf slowed down until it was walking beside the sleigh. Grandpère looked down at the strange wolf, and it looked back at him with its strange, glowing eyes. At that moment Grandpère realized that the creature was a loup-garou.

Then the creature spoke: "*Mon ami,* you must forgive my debt. Release me from the two dollars I owe you." With a start, Grandpère realized that the loup-garou was Henry, come to him at last to ask him to forgive the debt. Now Grandpère might have forgiven Henry in spite of his oath to the contrary if Henry had begged for his forgiveness or displayed deep sorrow over his debt. Your grandpère has a soft spot for people in need. But the loup-garou who had once been Henry did not sound sorry to your grandpère. He sounded arrogant and demanding, and that made your grandpère angry.

"I will not forgive your debt," Grandpère shouted at the loup-garou. "You can go to blazes!"

Grandpère urged his horse into a trot and drove briskly toward home, ignoring the loup-garou pacing beside him. As they reached the edge of the woods, the loup-garou said, "Release me from the two dollars I owe you."

"No!" shouted Grandpère, whipping his horse to a gallop. The poor horse was trembling with fear and exhaustion, but it obeyed his command and the sleigh fairly flew over the moonlit snow. The loup-garou flew beside it. As they drew near to the house, the loup-garou cried again, "Release me from the two dollars I owe you!" Once again your grandpère refused to forgive his debt.

Grandpère pulled up in front of the barn and unhitched his poor horse, which had grown resigned to its fate and stood still in spite of the presence of the huge wolf sitting beside the barn door. The loup-garou was watching every move your grandpère made with its huge, glowing eyes.

"*Mon ami,* you must forgive my debt," the loup-garou said softly. "Release me from the two dollars I owe you."

"I will not forgive your debt," said Grandpère stubbornly. "You can go to blazes!"

Grandpère led the terrified horse into the barn, and the loup-garou followed them inside and leaped into a manger. Grandpère put the horse into a stall at the far end of the barn and walked back to where the loup-garou crouched in the hay. For a long moment, your very stubborn grandpère and the very stubborn loup-garou stood eye-to-eye and glared at one another. Then your foolish grandpère gave a snort of disgust, turned his back to the loup-garou, and walked toward the barn door. That's when the wolf struck. It leaped from the manger, knocking your grandpère to the floor of the barn, and its teeth closed on your grandpère's neck, though it did not break his skin.

"Release me from the two dollars I owe you," growled the loup-garou.

Your grandpère was terrified. He was sure the loup-garou meant to kill him. Suddenly, his stubborn pride broke and he cried, "I release you from your two dollars. Now go to blazes and leave me in peace!"

At his words, the loup-garou vanished in a flash of light. Trembling with fear and rage, Grandpère stood up and marched out of the barn and into the house. I looked up when he came in, and he stalked over to my chair. I didn't know then what had happened to him, but I could see he was in a tizzy about something. "I hope you are satisfied!" he said to me. "I have forgiven old Henry his debt. But not until his loup-garou had me by the neck!"

Then he showed me his collar, which was ripped in half from the wolf's teeth, and your grandpère's neck was covered with the white froth from the creature's mouth.

After that your grandpère was never quite as stubborn. But it took a loup-garou to soften him.

25

Aunty Greenleaf and the White Deer

BROOKHAVEN, LONG ISLAND

Mama always told us to stay away from Aunty Greenleaf, though she never said why. Aunty Greenleaf was a scrawny old woman with a wild thatch of gray hair and a crooked nose. She lived in a hut surrounded by pines and catbriars just outside Brookhaven, and she sold herbal remedies to the folks in town. Mostly people avoided her, except when someone got sick.

My sister, Judith, and I (my name is Abe) were terribly curious about Aunty Greenleaf, but we didn't learn more about her until I was old enough to go to school. Then the other boys told me some stories about the old lady that made my skin crawl! Aunty Greenleaf was a witch, they said. She worked with herbs and other strange plants, and her home remedies worked too well to be natural. Folks figured she had to have help from the devil or one of his familiars. People said she had hexed a farmer's pigs once after he spoke rudely to her and they all died, one right after another. Then there was the time Mistress Williams dreamed of Aunty Greenleaf, and the

171

next morning her daughter fell ill with a fever and nearly died.

"If you drop a silver coin in her path, Aunty Greenleaf will turn around and walk away," Tommy said.

"Why?" I asked curiously.

Tommy shook his head sadly at my ignorance. "Because," he said, "a witch cannot pass anything made of silver. Everyone knows that, Abe!"

"Tell Abe about the witches' frolic, John," urged one of the older boys. John beckoned me closer, and we all huddled together.

"One night," John whispered, "Aunty Greenleaf and her witch friends crossed the Atlantic in an eggshell and frolicked with the witches in England! Then they magicked the eggshell so it brought them back here before sunrise."

The other boys nodded wisely. "Witchcraft!" they whispered.

I was a bit skeptical about the eggshell story. That didn't sound too likely to me. Mama says I take after my Pa, who only believes half of anything he hears in town. But I didn't say anything to the other boys.

I told Judith all about Aunty Greenleaf when I got home from school that day. She listened pop-eyed and made me promise never to cross the old lady, even if someone dared me to. Judith knows me too well!

A few months after I started school, folks in town began talking about a large, pure-white deer that was seen roaming the woods near Brookhaven at night. Several hunting parties were gathered to go after the large animal, but it seemed to be impervious to bullets, and folks began saying it was a phantom

AUNTY GREENLEAF AND THE WHITE DEER

deer. Around about that time, several women in the town began having trouble with their churning, and a number of cows and pigs began to sicken and die. Folks blamed the incidents on the phantom deer, though I noticed that each of the people afflicted with the trouble had crossed Aunty Greenleaf at some time in the last month. Aunty Greenleaf considered herself "sensitive" and took offense easily.

Pa laughed at the talk of a phantom deer. He got up a hunting party himself to chase down the animal. They were gone all day and well into the night. I heard him come in just before midnight, and I crept down the steps to listen to him tell Mama about the hunt.

"There really is a white deer," he said, sitting wearily in a chair to take off his boots. "Largest deer I have ever seen, and fast, too. We couldn't keep up with it. I got several good shots in, and I swear at least one of them hit the deer, but it just kept running. I have never seen anything like it."

Mama set a steaming bowl of stew in front of him, and they spoke for a long time about the white deer. I grew tired after a while and crept back to bed, wondering if the deer really was a phantom. *Or,* I mused, just before falling asleep, *what if it were a witch?* Witches sometimes transformed themselves into cats. Why not a deer? I thought of Aunty Greenleaf and then decided I was being foolish.

Pa became obsessed with the white deer. Every moment he could spare from his work, Pa would take his gun and go hunting in the woods around town. He saw the white deer several times, but his shots always seemed to go astray. We were getting worried about him. He wasn't sleeping well. Every night he was

plagued with horrible nightmares. He would wake up, screaming in terror and shouting aloud in a language none of us had
ever heard. Judith claimed she heard the name "Greenleaf"
among the foreign words. Pa had dark circles under his eyes and
his hands shook all the time. But he was still determined to
track and kill the white deer. Mama wanted to ask the minister
to pray over our house and banish whatever evil spirit was keeping Pa from his sleep, but Pa wouldn't hear of it.

Judith and I were both sure that Aunty Greenleaf was
behind Pa's nightmares and that it was she who roamed the
woods at night in the form of a white deer. One afternoon, I
saw Pa leaving the barn with his gun over his shoulder. I ran
out to him.

"Pa," I called, beckoning to Judith who had just come out
of the house. "May we speak to you?"

Pa smiled wearily at me and Judith. "I have been neglect-
ing you lately," he said, tousling my hair. "I am sorry about
that, Abe. The white deer seems to be all I can think about."

"That's why we wanted to speak to you," cried Judith,
hurrying up to us.

"We know you don't believe in phantoms, Pa," I said, "but
we think that the white deer really is supernatural."

"We think that if you use silver bullets, you can kill the
white deer," Judith added.

"Silver bullets?" asked Pa with a grin. "Do you think the
white deer is a witch?"

"We think you should use silver bullets," I repeated, ignoring his question. Pa didn't believe in witches any more than he
believed in phantoms.

Pa looked down into our pleading faces and gave in, as we knew he would.

"All right," he said. "If I don't kill the white deer today, the next time I hunt it, I will use silver bullets."

Judith and I were satisfied. Pa always kept his promises to us. Judith and I went inside and told Mama about our idea of using silver bullets to hunt the white deer. Mama thought this was a brilliant notion, and when Pa returned home after dark without the white deer, she reminded him of his promise to us.

After chores the next day, I saw Pa melting silver to make bullets. Then he took his gun and went out hunting the white deer. Mama let Judith and me wait up for Pa, since it was our idea to use silver bullets to shoot the white deer. It was long past our bedtime when Pa came in the door.

"Did you get the deer?" we all asked together.

"I got three shots in," Pa said, hanging his gun over the mantle. "The white deer actually stumbled as if one of the shots had hit it. Then it jerked upright and ran away. I tracked it almost to Aunty Greenleaf's hut, but it disappeared. I lost it in the dark somehow, which is mighty strange, seeing as the deer is pure white. I plan to go back there tomorrow morning to see if I can find it."

We were disappointed that our scheme had not turned out as we planned. Mama hurried us to bed, but she woke us early so we could wave good-bye to Pa as he left to search for the body of the white deer. Pa came home in the afternoon without the deer. He must have missed it after all, he told us. He stayed home the next two nights, his desire to hunt the white deer abated after the fiasco with the silver bullets. His nightmares had ceased after that night, and he seemed content to work on the farm and help me with my schoolwork.

Later that week Pa went into town. When he got home he looked unusually pale and upset.

"What's wrong?" Mama asked him, clutching at her heart with one hand. Pa looked as if something dreadful had happened. Judith and I pressed ourselves close to Mama, afraid of what Pa might say.

"I just heard in town that Aunty Greenleaf was taken ill several days ago," Pa said slowly. "Ever since she took sick, the farm animals have stopped dying and the families who have had trouble with their churning are back to normal. Aunty Greenleaf died this morning, and the doctor who cared for her told the minister he found three silver bullets in her spine!"

Judith and I looked at each other and nodded knowingly. So Aunty Greenleaf really was a witch. We had been right.

After the death of Aunty Greenleaf, the phantom white deer was never heard of or seen again in Brookhaven.

26

Van Wemple's Goose

BROOKLYN

If ever a man was henpecked, that man was Nicholas Van Wemple. He was a stout, round little fellow with a beaming smile and all the energy of a cat sleeping next to a good fire. He was quite well-to-do, but Vrouw Van Wemple held the purse strings, and she did not give him so much as one English shilling to spend on schnapps. Nicholas was rather hurt by this frugality, but he was too lazy to do anything about it. Vrouw Van Wemple had industry enough for three people, and she divided it equally between cleaning her house from top to bottom and scolding her phlegmatic husband in as shrill a tone as ever a hen used on her rooster.

Now around about Christmastime of the year 1739, a new rumor spread through Flatbush. Folks began saying the old tide mill was haunted. Mysterious lights would float around the mill in the middle of the night. Some men walking home from the tavern one evening had heard voices coming out of nowhere, and then they heard the terrible shrieking of a ghoul. It had scared them sober, so horrible was the cry. People started avoiding the tide mill after dark.

Vrouw Van Wemple scoffed at the stories of the supernatural and forbade Nicholas to talk to any of the men who had heard the unearthly scream of the ghoul. "Drunkards, the lot of them," his good Vrouw screeched at him, waving a dust cloth under his nose and making him sneeze. "And you would spend all our money on schnapps, just like the rest of those good-for-nothings if I would let you, Nicholas!"

"Of course I would not, my dear," Nicholas lied with a beaming smile. Folks in Flatbush could never figure out what Nicholas saw in his wiry-haired, double-chinned, red-faced wife, but he was as enamored with her after twenty henpecked years of marriage as he was the day they took their vows.

On New Year's Eve Vrouw Van Wemple reluctantly counted out ten English shillings into her husband's hand and sent him to fetch a fat goose from Dr. Beck. "Do not stop at the tavern, Nicholas Van Wemple," she screeched at him as he clapped on his hat and meandered out the door. "That money is for the goose, do you hear! Not for schnapps!"

Nicholas blew his bride a kiss and strolled down the icy road toward Dr. Beck's house, humming happily to himself. As he passed the tavern, a roguish breeze snatched his hat from his round head and blew it in the open door. Nicholas went to fetch his hat and was hailed at once by several of his friends. Smelling schnapps and tobacco, Nicholas beamed with delight and slid into a chair. *Now this was really something,* thought he, forgetting the goose entirely. He ordered up a schnapps, was treated to a second by his friends, and bought everyone a third round. As his pile of English shillings disappeared into the till, his friends laughingly asked him what his Vrouw thought of his night on the town. Nicholas grinned good-naturedly and said, "Well now, 'tis my money any way you look at it."

"That's not what my wife says," chuckled his next-door neighbor.

The warm bar and the schnapps were making Nicholas rather sleepy, so he laid his head down for a quick snooze. He woke with a start an hour later. His friends had all left the tavern, and the only voices he heard came from the next room. Two sailors with leather jackets, black beards, and earrings were talking together in low voices. Nicholas listened rather sleepily for a moment before he realized they were discussing some gold that had been buried in the cellar of the old tide mill. The two men finished their drinks hastily and hurried out of the tavern.

Nicholas left the bar slowly, his mind still in a haze from all the alcohol he had consumed. Only one thing was clear to him in his advanced state of inebriation: He had spent all his money on schnapps and had no goose to take home to his Vrouw. *This is not a good thing*, he mused. He decided that he should visit the tide mill in hopes of retrieving the gold and fetching home the goose before his wife learned about his latest escapade at the tavern.

Sneaking into the shed behind his house, Nicholas found an old shovel and a lantern. Then he marched as fast as his stout body and fat legs would take him to the decrepit old tide mill in the marshes. He hesitated for a moment when he saw the tumble-down building looming dark against the white snow, remembering the rumors of floating lights and unearthly shrieks. But the hope of gold urged him into the creaking dark-

VAN WEMPLE'S GOOSE

ness of the mill and down the wobbly stairs to the old cellar.

The earth of the cellar had not yet frozen, so it turned easily under Nicholas's shovel. Soon the tip of the shovel hit something. Nicholas dug deeper and unearthed a canvas bag. As he hauled the bag out of the hole, a seam ripped and gold coins spilled all around him. This sudden wealth was beyond anything Nicholas had dreamed of! He began stuffing the legs of his breeches with coins, humming happily to himself and dreaming of the smile that would light the face of his good Vrouw when she saw the gift he brought her.

The tread of feet on the rickety stairs brought Nicholas to his senses. He turned just in time to see four scruffy sailors enter the cellar. Two of them he recognized from the tavern. The other two were strangers. The men blinked in the lantern light, looking at the hole, at the open bag of gold coins, and lastly at Nicholas. He stared back, realizing suddenly that these were pirates. *So it is buccaneers who have been haunting the old tide mill*, he thought cheerfully as they frog-marched him up the wobbly stairs, gold coins spilling out the bottom of his trousers with each step.

The pirates sat Nicholas down unceremoniously next to the small fire they had lit, pushed a glass of hot Hollands into his hands, and forced him to drink a toast to their pirate flag. As a general rule, Nicholas did not approve of pirating as a profession, but pirating that involved hot Hollands couldn't be all that bad, to his way of thinking. He cheerfully downed his drink in one gulp and then gave a shout of surprise when two of the pirates grabbed his stout, round form and pitched him out the window. Nicholas grabbed desperately at a bundle hanging from the window frame as he sailed through, trying to save himself. The frayed rope holding the round object broke, and Nicholas had just enough time to realize he was clutching a goose that the pirates had stolen from a neighboring farm before he landed in the water and the mud outside the tide mill.

Nicholas kicked his way to the surface of the pool, jumped out of the mud as fast as he could, and staggered through the ice and snow in the general direction of his home, clutching the goose to his chest as he ran. He was nearly home when the events of the evening, coupled with the Hollands and the schnapps, overwhelmed him and he fainted into a snowbank a few feet from his door.

He was awakened in the wee hours by the shrill tones of Vrouw Van Wemple, who had discovered him missing from their bed and had hurried to look for him. He gazed blurrily up into her rough, beloved face and wordlessly thrust the featherless goose into her arms. Mollified by this unexpected gesture, Vrouw Van Wemple hurried her husband into the house, pulling off his snow-covered garments and forcing him into warm, dry nightclothes. She even heated up some Hollands she had hidden away from him and put his feet into a hot-water bath before she demanded to know where he had been all this while.

Nicholas eagerly told his tale of schnapps, gold, pirates, and the goose. Vrouw Van Wemple did not believe a word of it. There had not been one gold shilling in his britches when she had removed them, nor any in his boots!

"You are drunk, old man," she scolded, kissing him on the forehead.

"If I am drunk, old woman, then how could I afford to bring you a goose?" asked Nicholas. "Ask any man at the tavern, and he will tell you I had not one shilling on me when I left!"

"I still say you dreamed the whole thing," said Vrouw Van Wemple. "Now finish up your Hollands and come to bed."

Nicholas obediently drank his second cup of hot Hollands of the night and then followed his good wife up the stairs.

He told his story to their New Year's guests the next day while they partook of the roasted goose, but none of them believed him. After dinner, the men walked with Nicholas out to the old tide mill to check for the pirates, but the mill was empty and not one glimmer of gold was left on the creaking stairs or in the dirt of the cellar. Ever after, the story was told with many a wink and a laugh at Nicholas's drunken fancy. But Nicholas didn't care. He noticed that after his encounter with the pirates on New Year's Eve, the mysterious lights and voices vanished forever from the tide mill.

And it is all on account of Van Wemple's goose, Nicholas chuckled to himself.

27

High Hat

ALLEGHENY REGION

You can see him at the water's edge some nights, silhouetted against the sunset. "The Undertaker" we call him, since he appears to be wearing a stovepipe hat above his craggy face, with a lank form and white gloves on his hands. He is a giant, tall as a tree, with a taste for human flesh. High Hat is his true name, and no one goes near him. He has been haunting the swamplands for more years than can be counted.

Folks who live near his section of the swamp tend to hang hunks of meat from the trees to discourage him from eating their livestock or stealing folks away. It seems to work pretty well, because only a few chickens and pigs go missing each year, and only one neighbor was stolen. That was a bad day all around when that happened. Fortunately, before he come to any harm, a group of armed men went into the swamp and fetched him out of the tree into which High Hat had stashed him.

No one knows exactly where High Hat came from origi-nally. The tale I favor myself is from the Iroquois, and it claims that High Hat is the last of the Stone Giants. The Stone Giants were fierce, tall creatures made of flesh and

185

blood, but their outer skin was as hard as stone. They lived near the Iroquois—at that time only five nations strong—and at first they seemed content to dwell in peace with their neighbors. Then one hard winter left the Stone Giants starving. To survive, they started eating the flesh of humans. This did not make them ideal neighbors, and there was conflict between the Iroquois and the Stone Giants. The Iroquois creator-god finally interceded in the conflict, disguising himself as a handsome Stone Giant and persuading the Stone Giants to unite in a war against the Iroquois. The army of giants camped for the night in a deep valley, and the creator-god started an avalanche that killed all but one of the Stone Giants, who escaped into the Allegheny hills. It's my theory that he finally settled in these swamplands, where he still hankers after human flesh.

I had only one encounter with High Hat, and that was one too many. I had some business with a farmer who lived on the far side of the marshlands just on the outskirts of High Hat's stomping grounds, and since it was a beautiful summer day I decided to walk rather than take the wagon. The farmer and I dickered over our business until sunset, when we finally agreed on a price for the horse I wanted to buy. We shook hands on the deal, and I promised to come by the next day with the money to pick up the horse.

The farmer's wife invited me in for supper, but I knew my wife was making shepherd's pie, which was my favorite, so I declined. The farmer and his wife exchanged uneasy glances, and the farmer asked me if he could drive me home in his wagon, since it was getting dark. "Don't want the Undertaker to take a bite out of you," he joked, but I could tell that underneath his levity he was serious.

"I'll be fine," I said, shaking off his offer of assistance. "I will see you tomorrow!"

I set out determinedly for home, not glancing back though I knew the farmer and his wife watched me worriedly until I was out of sight. *Folks who lived near High Hat's territory were always a bit cautious,* I thought as I turned onto the road through the swamp. The crickets, frogs, and other creatures were starting up their nightly clamor as I strolled along. It was a beautiful evening, and I was enjoying the walk and looking forward to my pie when I passed a close-growing stand of trees. A rotten smell drifted into my nostrils. I held my nose for a moment, gagging, and saw several hunks of meat trailing from the branches. I had forgotten all about High Hat after leaving the farm, but here was warning indeed against the flesh-eating swamp dweller.

For the first time, I felt uneasy. It was twilight and I couldn't see very well. I suddenly realized that the night creatures had fallen silent, and there was no sound but the rustle of a light breeze in the treetops. Or was it a breeze? I almost thought I saw the silhouette of a stovepipe hat with a craggy face beneath it just beyond the copse of trees. I decided it was my imagination, but I quickened my pace. I was still 2 miles from home, and I no longer fancied a walk in the dark. I kept listening for the croak of a frog, the chirp of a cricket, and other small night sounds that would signal all was well. There was only silence and the sound of my footsteps. I had the growing sense that something was keeping pace with me back in the trees, yet I did not hear any rustling of leaves like I had heard back at the copse of trees. My breath was coming unevenly now, and I walked still faster, staying at the center of the dirt road, watching the trees warily in the failing light, wishing I had taken the farmer up on his offer of a ride home.

The cracking of a stick under a large foot rang out like a shot, and I started running. I could hear the pounding of giant-sized feet as High Hat kept pace with me in the trees beside the swamp, no longer troubling to stay silent. The road curved ahead, and I raced to get to the curve before the giant creature, but suddenly he burst forth from the trees and grabbed me with his blood-stained, white-gloved hands. He had obviously been feasting on the farmers' offerings just as I happened past. He lifted me up, struggling, toward his craggy face, and I could smell the noxious fumes of his breath.

"Let me go," I shouted, pummeling him with my fists. I landed a good shot on his nose and then managed to poke my fist into his large eye. High Hat gave a howl of pain and dropped me abruptly, clutching at his eye. I rolled along the ground and dove under a low bramble bush at the edge of the road while the giant was distracted by pain.

A moment later, High Hat came looking for me, still clutching his blood-stained glove to his sore eye, muttering fiercely to himself in a language I did not understand, though his intent was very clear. He stomped up and down the road, beating at the bushes with a limb he tore from one of the trees. Twice he passed the bramble bush where I lay, and the branch slammed the brambles deep into my flesh. Blood was oozing through my shirt, and I did not know if I could take

HIGH HAT

another beating like that without screaming and giving away my position.

Suddenly, I heard the jingling of a horse's harness and the clip-clop of a horse's hooves as it trotted down the road, pulling a wagon. A light appeared in the distance, coming from the direction of the farmhouse I had left less than half an hour before. I heard the howl of a hound dog, which was swiftly taken up by a second as they caught the scent of High Hat ahead of them. The giant creature glared toward the light, tapping the tree branch once, twice against its blood-stained, gloved hand. Then it tossed the branch aside and faded into the woods near the swamp, thankfully on the opposite side of the road from my hiding place. I could still see his silhouette clearly near the edge of the water, until the lantern light from the wagon dazzled my eyes.

I did not emerge from my hiding place until the farmer's wagon was almost beside me. Then I scrambled out of the brambles and was astride the wagon in two bounds, and up next to the farmer in three. The dogs were in the back of the wagon. They alternated between growls and whimpers as they stared toward the place where High Hat was concealed. The farmer didn't say a word. He just whipped up his horse and drove me home as fast as we could go. We didn't slow down until we turned into my barnyard.

My wife came out of the house to greet us, and she gasped in horror when she saw what a bleeding mess I was.

"Best to get him in the house, missus, and get him some brandy," the farmer advised her. "He's had a nasty encounter with High Hat and will need some medical attention and rest."

I was still too shocked to speak. I nodded my thanks to the farmer and limped into the house, leaning against my wife's shoulder. She filled me up with brandy, pulled the thorns out of my mangled back, and bandaged me up. Then she brought the shepherd's pie to the fireside where I lay dozing in shock and pain, and she made me eat every bite before I told her my story. She scolded me soundly for walking alone at dusk through High Hat territory and ended up in tears, blessing the farmer who had saved my life.

The farmer came by the next morning with my new horse, sparing me the necessity of traveling back along the road where I had had such a narrow escape. He made me swear to him that I would never again venture near High Hat territory alone at night, and I promised willingly.

I have been content ever since to view "the Undertaker" from a distance, much to the relief of my wife.

28

The Ramapo Salamander

ROCKLAND COUNTY

I remember very little of my early childhood, though much I have to relate stems directly from the events that took place at that time. My older brother and I were born in Germany to a nobleman named Hugo. My mother was a good and pious woman who named me Mary after the mother of our Savior. In those days, it was her purity that kept my father from straying too far into the love of wealth.

My brother and I were very small when we sailed to the New World with our parents. We settled in the Ramapo Mountains near High Tor, sometimes called Torn Mountain. At the time, there was a story circulating through our community regarding this holy place. It was said that Amasis, the third of the magi who had once followed the Star of Bethlehem, had traveled through Asia and across the vast northern expanses of this land and had settled on Torn Mountain. He took to himself a native wife, with whom he had one child. Amasis had built a temple on top of the mountain in worship of the one true God, and to him was revealed the secret of wealth that lay in the rocks under the mountain.

Now Amasis had refused to acknowledge the religion of the local tribes, and they hated him for it. While his wife lived, Amasis was safe, for she was beloved of her people. After she died, their hatred of the foreigner caused the men of the tribe to attack him and his daughter. But God sent a mighty earthquake that opened up a new channel in the Hudson River, and the tribesmen were swallowed up by the earth. Only Amasis and his daughter survived.

My father, Hugo, built a forge and he did good business in this new land. In the old country, it was the custom that every seven years the fires of the forge were allowed to go out. This was to discourage earth elementals such as the salamander from gaining strength from the unquenched flame. My father laughed at such superstitious tales and refused to allow his workers to quench the fire of the forge.

My mother once told my brother and me about earth elementals. They were the spirits of fallen angels, who for love of the senses had abandoned their holy form to dwell among mankind, tempting them and making mischief. For their evil deeds, they had been bound to the earth, unable to leave it unless a human loosed them or they voluntarily passed a series of trials that would restore them to a redeemed state and send them back to God.

Mother was very apprehensive about the unquenched forge, and as the seventh year drew to a close, she succumbed to a high fever from worry and stress. I do not think Father realized how much his stubborn refusal to put out the forge had affected her. He loved her dearly and paid handsomely for the best doctors to treat her condition. But she was still confined to her bed, too weak to move, on the first day of the eighth year, when Father left us to go to work at the forge.

I have long since blocked out all memory of that terrible day, and so it was my nursemaid, Marta, who later told me what had happened. When my father entered the forge, he found all of his men gathered around the fire, mesmerized by a glowing figure deep within it. The figure seemed to be made of flame, and it was bobbing its head, darting its tongue in and out, and moving its tail back and forth. As my father approached, its tail whipped out and scorched a hole into the stone floor. My father stood transfixed by the creature, which was one of the legendary fire salamanders.

Unbeknownst to my father, my mother had risen from her sickbed. She knew that something evil would happen that day because of the unquenched fire. She went to the church and took some holy water from the font. Then she followed my father to the forge. When she saw the salamander, my mother threw the entire bowl of holy water into the forge, chanting an old German incantation she had learned from her granny. As the droplets brushed my father's face, he snapped out of his trance in time to catch his wife as she fainted.

A peal of thunder shook the building and a great storm roared above the town, with fearsome lightning flashing through the clouds and torrents of rain pouring down. Floodwater swirled into the forge, sweeping everyone into the corners of the room as it quenched the fire. When the storm ceased—as abruptly as it had started—the salamander was gone and my mother was dead.

I was nine years old when my mother died, and from that

THE RAMAPO SALAMANDER

time on, my father was a grim-faced, bitter man who blamed himself for his wife's death and grew infuriated any time someone mentioned the salamander. For the salamander was not gone. Sometimes, on cold mornings, the men would see the salamander blinking at them in the fires of the forge. As soon as they spotted it, the salamander would whisk its tail at them and disappear in a fountain of sparks. People from our town claimed to have spotted the salamander at the top of High Tor at night, its light reflecting balefully up into the night sky directly above the location where, it was said, Amasis had built his temple. A few others claimed to have seen a strange boy with eyes that glowed like the flames of a salamander wandering the Ramapos.

To their credit, the townsfolk never chided my father for releasing a fire salamander into their midst. I believe they felt he had suffered enough when he lost my mother. They all watched me and my brother rather more closely, however, than they did other children our age. They were afraid that the salamander would be especially attracted to the children of the man who had set him free to roam the Ramapos, and they protected us as much as they could. Father was the worst of the lot. He would not allow my brother or me to set foot in his forge, and he even forbade us to walk in its vicinity.

Four years after the salamander's release, a terrible fire raged through the mountain near our home. Watching from the second-story window of our house, I could see the salamander dancing upon the flames that raced from tree to tree. The whole town worked day and night to quench the blaze before it reached us. Several of the men came so near the salamander that they could have touched it if they had so wished. Father locked my brother and me into our house for the duration of the fire, for he was determined that he would not lose anyone else to the salamander. We were not released until the last ashes of the fire had been cool for a week.

Seven years after the salamander began roaming our land, a special consecration ceremony for young people was scheduled to take place at the church in our town. Everyone was very excited about the ceremony. The church was decorated until you could barely see the pews, and all the young men and women participating in the ceremony made new clothes. Marta, who acted now as our housekeeper rather than our nursemaid, helped me make a dress of white silk. Father told me I looked like an angel of light when he saw me walking down the stairs the morning of the ceremony. My brother, too, looked handsome in his new garments, and they escorted me to church with all the pomp and circumstance due my elegant appearance.

"We shall soon have to worry about beaus," my brother teased me gently. "We will need to keep a club near the front door to discourage them."

We all laughed at my brother's nonsense. I remember that moment so clearly even now, for it was the very last time I heard my father laugh.

At the close of the ceremony, all the young people in the town knelt before the altar at the front of the church while the minister blessed us. I had my head bowed in an attitude of reverence, and it took me a moment to register the sudden brightening of the light in the church. I opened my eyes quickly, startled at the glare, and saw the salamander floating just above the flames of the candelabra next to the altar. The congregation gasped at the sight of the evil creature, and the minister raised his prayer book in both hands, holding it between himself and the salamander in a gesture of defiance.

Just for a moment my eyes met the glowing eyes of the salamander. Then it switched its flaming tale and disappeared with a bang. At the same moment, a streak of fire blasted forth from the candelabra, throwing me backward with its force. It struck my brother, who was kneeling beside me. For a moment, I saw him outlined in flame. Then he disappeared as completely as the salamander had, never to be seen again.

The church was in chaos, women screaming, men shouting, the young men and women who had been kneeling in front of the altar running frantically away, fearing for their lives. I lay where I had fallen, my white dress scorched so badly I was barely decent, my long blonde hair falling from its pins. I stared at the spot where my brother had knelt a moment before, unable to move, unable to take in what I had just witnessed. I heard a sudden cry of anguish and tore my gaze from the altar to look out into the church. My father had risen from his pew and was staring at the burnt spot in front of the altar where my brother had been. He took two great strides forward and then fainted dead away. He did not revive to his pain for many hours.

After my brother's death, my father changed. He became obsessed with both the gaining of wealth, which I believe he thought might help fill the emptiness in his heart, and the destruction of the salamander, who had cost him a wife and son. I was the only person who could make my father smile and increasingly, the only one my father could bear to speak with for more than five minutes at a time. He spent many long hours at the forge, and when he was not at the forge he was concocting wild business investments, some of which worked, most of which did not. He refused to set foot in the church where my brother had been killed, questioning the piety of a minister who would allow an evil salamander to appear at the altar. He tried to forbid me the church, but I was old enough to make up my own mind, and I told him so. Reluctantly, he allowed me to attend for the sake of my good mother, who would have been horrified if her children did not go to church.

And thus another seven years passed away. I was a woman grown, and I did have many beaus, as my beloved brother had predicted. There were none who caught my fancy, however, until a young man named Justin, with a darkly handsome face and noble bearing, came to town and took work at my father's forge. Justin quickly showed his expertise at the forge. He had an incredible tolerance for the heat of the fire that allowed him to do work the others could not. He advanced quickly in the trade, and my father befriended him and brought him often to our home for dinner. Though Justin never officially joined the ranks of my beaus, there was a great deal of unspoken feeling between us, and I hoped that one day soon he would speak to me of matters more tender than those of work and the town.

During this time, my father began to leave the forge in Justin's keeping, and he often ventured afield, hiking through the woods and over the mountains to I knew not where. Sometimes he would stay out for a day and a night, which wor-

The earth elementals took up their calls urgently, begging my father to free them and offering him all the riches in the cavern if he would just speak the holy words inscribed on the back of the salamander. Since turning his back on the church my father had lost his ability to understand the holy tongue, so he bade me read the words on the salamander's back, for he was convinced that the words would teach him how to enter the depths and retrieve the riches below. I read aloud the words of the warning but refused to tell my father the other words that would free the earth elementals to work their evil upon mankind. My father was so angry that he raised his hand as if to strike me down where I stood. I cowered before him, afraid of my father for the first time in my life. The look on my face stopped him. His arm fell to his side, and then he gasped "Forgive me, Mary," and buried his face in his hands.

Silently I led him from the bewitched cavern, followed by the light of the salamander, which had grown brilliant with the reading of the words on its back. The salamander's glow lit our way through the dark night. When I glanced back over my shoulder, I could see the light blazing from the top of High Tor.

Many nights thereafter, my father left the house at dusk to return to High Tor. He would enter the magical cavern and try to read the writing on the salamander's back, but without success. On those nights, I would see the bright light of the salamander blazing again from the top of the mountain, and I would pray to God to break my father's obsession with the wealth the cavern contained.

My distress over my father was depriving me of appetite, so that Marta scolded me each day and the cook made special dinners to tempt me. I tired of their coddling, and one afternoon I slipped away and went for a long walk in the woods, trying to find some serenity from the beauty around me. I was startled by the sudden growl of a large cat and saw a panther crouched on a limb above me, ready to pounce. I screamed and fled, the panther close on my heels. I heard an answering shout, followed by the sharp report of a rifle. The panther fell dead at my feet. I stared down at the cat in horror, my body shaking with terror and shock, and then looked up into the face of my rescuer. It was Justin.

He was almost as pale as I was. I fell into his arms and cried out my shock and terror. He stroked my hair, murmuring gently to me until I calmed down. When at last I looked up into his face, I saw such a look of tenderness upon it that I realized without a shadow of doubt that he returned my affection. I opened my mouth to speak, but he put me from him.

"Hush, my dear. We do not have much time," Justin said. "I have many things to tell you. You may think, my beautiful Mary, that you love me. But know that I came to you in my elemental form and placed a magic crown of jewels from the cavern on High Tor upon your brow so that you would fall in love with me."

I stared at him blankly, trying to understand his words. Was he claiming to be one of the elementals from Amasis's cavern? How could that be?

"What I did not expect," Justin continued, "was that I would fall in love with you in return. But your gentleness, your piety, and your love for your father have filled me with a hope that I had long forgotten. The hope of redemption."

A sudden, terrible thought struck me. This wonderful man who had just saved me from the panther, could he be the salamander in disguise? Please God, no, I prayed, sensing even as I prayed that this was the truth.

"Justin," I whispered his name pleadingly.

"Hear me out, Mary," he said. "We are almost out of time. Alone, I have walked the darkness of this universe, and my desire for the things of this earth has bound me for many years. You are redeemed, but my redemption was in peril because of my love of the senses. The only way we can ever be together, the only way I can return to God, is to pass a series of trials that will restore me to a redeemed state. Long ago, I grew weary of this earth and began working my way through these trials. I had only one trial left—the trial by fire—when I was tempted by Amasis's treasure beneath High Tor and the unquenched flame of your father's forge offered me the means to obtain it."

I gasped, my eyes filling with tears. This man *was* the salamander in human form! *He* was the one responsible for the death of my mother and my brother. I should hate this man! I should flee from him. But I could not. When I thought of the salamander, I was filled with revulsion. But the soul of the man who was Justin was the soul of one trying to break free from the evil creature the salamander had become, and him I could not hate.

In the distance, I could hear shouts and the sound of many feet traveling in our direction. Justin continued, speaking as rapidly as he could to finish his story before the men arrived. "When your mother poured holy water on me in the forge, it transformed me temporarily into the form of a male child. I was assaulted for the first time by the senses as they are experienced by a human, and I was overwhelmed. As quickly as I could, I transformed back into a salamander and made my way to the magic cavern on High Tor. But somehow, the wealth in the cavern did not satisfy me. I took to walking the Ramapo Mountains in my human guise, learning to eat, drink, sleep, and experience life as a man. I both hated and loved my new form. I longed to be a true human, but it was not in my grasp, for I had not been redeemed."

The voices were growing louder, and I could hear that they were hostile. But I had no attention to spare from Justin's story.

"Finally I grew angry with your family, because it was your mother who had caused me to lose my love of Amasis's treasure, for which I had long sought, and had forced upon me a human form that I could not keep. I took my revenge upon your brother, and later, upon you by causing you to fall in love with me. I intended to seduce you and then leave you shamed and scorned. But as I grew to know you, your purity pierced my heart. Many nights I would take the form of a true elemental and would sit on a moonbeam watching you sleep and wishing that I was a real human man who could woo and win you for my wife. I began to dream again of being redeemed. If I returned to God, then my soul would be fit for you, and I could be with you one day when you returned to His presence."

Justin reached up then and touched my head. A soft weight of which I had been totally unaware lifted from me as he removed the bewitched crown from my brow and threw it on the ground.

"You are free, Mary," he said.

I waited for a moment, wondering if the feelings I had for Justin would fall away from me as the crown had. I looked deep into his golden brown eyes and saw myself reflected there. I knew then that I was in his soul, and he in mine. I reached up and touched his face.

"I am not free," I said. "I have not been free from the day I first met you."

For a moment, his face lit up with joy as he realized what I was saying. He took my hand and kissed it, and then said urgently, "My dearest love, I cannot stay with you. I am not entitled to this form, and I have one trial left to claim my redemption. That trial I will stand today. About an hour ago, one of the men at the forge bumped into me and the back of my shirt ripped. In that moment, he saw the triangle branded on my back, and he spoke of it to your father. Now your father knows who I am, and he is following me with many men. I stand condemned for the murder of your brother and the death of your mother, and I will face my punishment as a man rather than resume my salamander form and live as an earth elemental. In so doing, I hope to prove myself worthy of redemption. And worthy of you."

As Justin spoke the last words, my father burst into the clearing where we stood, followed by many armed men. He sprang upon Justin, pulling him away from me, and tore the shirt from his back, revealing the triangle with which Justin, in his salamander form, had been branded.

"He has ruined my household," Father shouted, "and he should be thrown back into the forge from whence he came."

I gasped desperately, reaching out to Justin as he was bound by the men. Justin met my eyes, his face serene, and mouthed the words "I love you" to me just before the men dragged him back to town. I followed, dazed by grief and horror. When I stepped into the forge, my father caught my arm and tried to push me outside, but I wouldn't go. I watched them thrust Justin, my Justin, into the hot flames. I was trembling fiercely, but I was trying to be as brave as he was.

For a long moment I saw Justin's human form burning in the forge, and then it transformed briefly into the shape of the salamander before taking on the misty shape of an elemental. The elemental rose out of the forge, and as it reached the ceiling it transformed once again into the human man I had known as Justin. He was clothed now in silver robes, his face glorified. Our eyes met one last time, and then he rose straight through the ceiling. I ran outside and watched Justin rising up and up to disappear through the clouds.

"Go to God, my darling," I called softly through my tears. "I will be with you presently."

My father came out of the forge to stand beside me. He looked shaken, and he put his hand on my shoulder.

"The salamander that killed your brother is gone," he said softly. "But I believe that the soul of the man called Justin may have been saved."

I turned to look up at my father. "I know he was," I said softly.

I took his hand in mine, and we returned to our home.

29

The Flying Canoe

LAKE GEORGE

Maman was none too pleased when not one, but both of her French-Canadian daughters married American men and moved to the United States to live. Jillian married an architect named Greg, and they moved to Lake George in New York. I (my name is Marie) married Richard, and we moved to a small hamlet near the Saint Lawrence River.

My husband did not speak much French when we first met, but I gradually taught him. When Maman finally came to visit us, he chattered to her like a native of Quebec, which pleased her greatly. As a reward, she would tell him many stories that she had learned as a child. Richard's favorite story was about *la chasse galerie*—the Flying Canoe.

"Long ago," Maman told Richard, "but not so long ago, there were a number of lonely lumberjacks working in the center of a very large forest. They cut down mammoth trees and watched them crash into the thick snow in exactly the place where they said the trees would land. They would cut up the trees and haul them hither and thither. They worked hard, *mon Dieu*, very hard indeed! But they were lonely for the women they had left behind."

Richard sat on a stool beside the kitchen counter, listening enthralled to the tale as Maman made dinner. Maman placed a cutting board and some carrots and celery in front of him, and he automatically started chopping them up for salad while she continued her story.

"On New Year's Day it snowed so hard no work could be done. The men huddled in their camp and spoke longingly of their home. They passed around the rum and drank toasts to the New Year, but finally a lumberjack named Baptiste said what they were all thinking: 'I wish to go home today and see my girl!' There were murmurs of agreement, but Jean replied: 'How can we go home today? There are more than 2 meters of snow on the road, and more snow is falling. You are crazy, Baptiste.'"

I took the chopped vegetables away from Richard before he made them too small and mixed them in with the rest of the salad.

"What happened next?" asked Richard, hardly noticing that the vegetables were gone. Maman smiled at him and continued her tale.

"'Who said we were *walking* out of here?' asked Baptiste. 'I am going to paddle out in my canoe.'

"Now the men all knew that Baptiste had a canoe with paddles out back of the camp. Baptiste had made a pact with the devil. If the devil would make the canoe fly wherever Baptiste wished, Baptiste would not pray the Mass for an entire year. And if Baptiste did not return the canoe before dawn of the day after he used it, the devil could keep his soul. While Baptiste was in *la chasse galerie,* he could not say the name of

God or fly over a church or touch any crosses, or the canoe would crash."

Maman paused to put something in the oven, and then said, "Many of the men refused to participate in Baptiste's New Year's scheme, but he managed to find seven companions to fly with him in the canoe back to their hometown to visit their women. Baptiste and his friends got into the canoe, and Baptiste pronounced the magic words: 'Caïdemór Lerricht! Caïdemór Lerricht! Caïdemór Lerricht!' " When he was done binding himself to the devil, the canoe rose into the air and the men began to paddle their way through the sky to their home. Their womenfolk were so glad to see them! They celebrated long into the night, drinking and dancing. It was close to dawn when the men realized they had to return the canoe to the lumbercamp by dawn or forfeit their souls.

"They searched for Baptiste and found him as drunk as a lord lying under a table at the inn. They bundled him into the canoe, spoke the magic words, and paddled away.

Knowing that Baptiste would start swearing if they woke him, one of the men tied him up and gagged him so he would not speak the name of God at an inopportune moment and crash the canoe. When Baptiste awoke, he sat up, struggling with the ropes that bound him. He managed to loosen the gag and shouted, 'Mon Dieu, why have you tied me up?' At the name of God, the canoe took a nosedive, plunging toward the ground. It hit the top of a large pine tree, and all the men tumbled out and fell down into the darkness just before dawn. They were never seen again!"

Richard gave a sigh of delight. "What a marvelous story,"

THE FLYING CANOE

he said, and kissed Maman on the cheek. Maman giggled and blushed like a schoolgirl.

I was expecting our first child at the time, and soon after Maman returned home, Richard was sent to Quebec on a business trip of several weeks' duration. I was four weeks from my delivery date and a bit nervous about staying alone with the baby almost due, so Richard arranged for me to stay with my sister and her husband at their home in Lake George while he was away. He assured me that he would be home long before the baby was born. Comforted by his promise, I packed my bag and drove down to be with my sister.

Jillian and Greg welcomed me with open arms. Jillian cooked special meals to tempt my failing appetite, and Greg set up a comfortable seat for me out in the backyard, where I could put up my feet and look out over the lake. I spoke to Richard on his cell phone each evening, and he told me about his travels and how many folks mistook him for a native of Quebec. It was a peaceful time that was dispelled suddenly when I went into labor three weeks early. The pains were ten minutes apart, and the local doctor told me to stay at the house until they were closer to five minutes apart. I was distraught. Richard was somewhere in the north of Quebec, and I was sure he would not make it to Lake George in time to see our baby born. I called him and told him the news, and he promised to drive home as fast as he could.

I sat outside with Jillian, trying to stay as relaxed as I could between labor pains. My contractions were only eight minutes apart when Richard phoned from a little north country pub to tell me the car had broken down. I lost it then and started sobbing on the phone. I tried to be brave, knowing Richard felt terrible about missing the birth of our son, but I couldn't help crying. I hung up slowly and went back outside to walk up and down the yard, hoping that the walking would make the baby come faster.

About an hour later, as I sat in my comfortable chair sipping water and trying to ignore the contractions, which continued steadily at eight minutes, I caught sight of something flying low over the horizon. I didn't hear the sound of an engine, and the shape of the object was unlike any airplane I had ever seen.

"What is that?" I asked Jillian. She shaded her eyes and then went inside to get her binoculars. She focused on the object for a moment and then dropped the binoculars in shock.

"It's *la chasse galerie!*" she exclaimed. "And Richard is inside it with seven other men!"

"What!" I cried, snatching up the binoculars from the ground and focusing them on the flying object. She was right. Richard was sitting in the front of a flying canoe, paddling as fast as he could. He was accompanied by seven seedy characters who looked as if the majority of their lives were spent in bars. The canoe was getting large and larger as it sailed toward us above the lake. As it drew near, Richard spotted Jillian and me standing on the lawn at the back of her house.

"*Mon Dieu*, Marie!" he shouted. "Shouldn't you be at the hospital?"

At the name of God, the canoe shuddered to a halt and then tipped forward, dumping Richard out the front end. He

plunged into the lake and came up sputtering with indignation. The men in the boat laughed uproariously at Richard, and then grabbed their paddles and began chanting some foreign-sounding words that sounded ominously close to those Maman had chanted in her story. The canoe began flying forward again, and *la chasse galerie* disappeared over the treetops.

Richard swam to shore as fast as he could and stumbled, dripping and swearing, up onto the dock just as Greg came outside to find out what all the shouting was about.

"Good lord, Richard, where did you drop from?" Greg asked in astonishment. Jillian and I burst out laughing. Richard made a growling noise and came up to me. "Why aren't you at the hospital?" he demanded in a grumpy tone.

"Because the contractions are still eight minutes apart," I explained soothingly.

"The doctor doesn't want Marie to come in until the contractions are five minutes apart," Jillian explained as I tried to breathe through another contraction.

"We'd best get you out of those wet clothes," said Greg to my husband, "or they won't let you into the hospital." He led Richard to the house, and as the door closed behind him, I heard Greg ask, "How did you manage to get here so quickly? An hour ago, Marie told us you had broken down."

I didn't hear Richard's reply, because a second contraction had swiftly followed the first.

"I think it's time to go," I told my sister.

Our son was born several hours later, and it wasn't until everyone else had gone home and Richard, baby Nathan, and I were alone that I asked him about *la chasse galerie*.

"When I stopped at the pub to phone you about the car," Richard explained, "Several of the men were talking about how lousy the beer was. A man there suggested flying down to a great pub he knew near Lake George. When I heard they were flying to Lake George, I told them about the baby and asked if I could join them. I thought they were talking about an airplane. You could have knocked me over with a feather when they pulled out a canoe, pushed me into the front seat, and started paddling it up into the sky, just the way Maman described in her story. I tell you, Marie, it was the fastest and smoothest flight I have ever taken! Maybe the airlines should invest in a fleet of canoes!"

"I still don't believe what happened, and I saw you with my own two eyes," I exclaimed. "Still, it makes me rather uneasy. If the folktales are true, then that canoe was powered by the devil. I don't want my son growing up with a father who owes his soul to Satan. You'd better go to church right away and pray to *le bon Dieu* to save your soul, just in case."

That's just what Richard did.

30

Jan Sol and the Monster

WALL STREET, MANHATTAN

Back in the days when the Dutch occupied the isle of Manhattan and Wall Street had a wall, there lived a square-built, pop-eyed, flat-faced soldier named Jan Sol, who was (by his own reckoning at least) the bravest man in the garrison. He was a corporal in the town guard, and he spent many a night escorting drunks home from the tavern—if they were wealthy—or to the lockup if they were not. He also kept the wastrels inside the town and the Indians outside of it, and made sure no unlawful entry was made into any of the good Dutchmen's houses.

One fine Saturday night in early spring, Jan Sol was assigned to guard the gate located on the present-day Wall Street. He paced up and down vigilantly for at least ten minutes before he put down his blunderbuss and leaned lazily against the wall to take a quick rest. The sounds of the night filled his ears, and his thoughts were not pleasant ones. There had been talk of witches lately. It was rumored that they had arrived in the New World, and many a strange and sinister happening was reckoned to their credit. Terrible, shapeless forms were encountered by a few women in the Ladies' Alley, and there was a report of a large, fast-growing clump of toadstools in Windmill Meadow that had sprung up overnight.

It was, Jan Sol suddenly realized, a very eerie sort of night. The trees whispered and snickered and snapped in the wind. Shadows flitted back and forth before his eyes. One shadow had long fingers, like an oversized hand. The fingers seemed to beckon to him, moving slowly in a nightmarish rhythm. A short shriek came from the woods. Jan Sol shivered and grabbed his blunderbuss before he realized it was only an owl.

A few paces away, the windmill began to turn and creak. Jan whipped around and threatened it with his blunderbuss for a moment. He laughed shakily when he realized what was causing the sound and lowered his gun. He pulled out his flask of schnapps with shaking hands, lifted it to his lips, and took a long pull. As he drank, he caught a glimpse of something large and black over the top of his flask. He dropped it with a gasp as a terrible monster with long teeth, thrashing wings, and horrible, glowing eyes came charging at the wall. Jan fumbled for his blunderbuss and fired a shot at the creature. The blunderbuss was heavily loaded, and it knocked Jan flat. Jan stared up at the starry sky, his heart pounding furiously. He expected the monster to pounce on him at any moment, but all he heard was the excited shouts of the relief guard, who came running when they heard the shot.

The relief guard picked Jan Sol up and carted him, limp and shaking, to the governor. The governor, roused from a sound sleep, was not pleased to hear Jan Sol's story of a monster. Smelling the schnapps on his breath, the governor warned

JAN SOL AND THE MONSTER

him against overindulgence and sentenced him to four hours riding the wooden horse in full view of the town.

"I am being punished?" Jan Sol shrieked. "For what? Protecting the good people from a monster?"

The governor waved him away with a frown and went back to his bed. The next morning Jan Sol was put on the wooden horse and forced to ride up and down the streets, much to the amusement of the good people and his fellow officers. When his punishment was finished, he was brought before the council, wincing and thumping his legs to get the circulation going, and the council listened gravely to his tale of the monster that had attacked the gate in the night. Several hours were spent discussing the monster and what should be done about it. The meeting adjourned abruptly after a taciturn member of the council asked dryly, "Are we sure there *is* a monster?" It was decided to wait and see if the monster made another appearance before spending more time debating the matter.

The next Saturday night, six men joined Jan Sol at the gate on Wall Street. They were loaded down with iron weights borrowed from various shopkeepers, so that the monster would not fly off with them if and when it made an appearance. After standing guard all in a row from dusk until midnight, the guardsmen agreed to take turns watching the gate. They drew straws, and the short straw fell to Jan Sol. He turned pale but bravely went to stand watch as his fellow guardsmen went to sleep in the lee of the wall.

The moon was setting and darkness settled over the earth. The wind picked up and the windmill began to creak and groan, as it had the night the monster first appeared. Jan felt his heart begin to pound. Then he heard the thud of foot-steps—large footsteps—and suddenly an awful figure with flut-tering wings rose above the timber fort. Jan froze in his tracks, watching in horror as the monster flew down from the top of the fort, glided swiftly toward the house of the governor, and leaped the wall, easily avoiding the broken bottles strewn around to defend it.

Jan Sol suddenly found his voice and gave a yell that instantly woke his fellow guardsmen. It took the trembling, stuttering Jan a good quarter of an hour to tell his story. When they finally realized that the monster had returned, the alarmed guardsmen stormed to the governor's home and roused the household.

While the governor was being informed of the threat to his household, two guardsmen heard the sound of stealthy foot-steps approaching the gate from inside the wall of the gover-nor's house. The men flattened themselves on either side of the gate and held a rope across it. There was the sound of a key turning in the lock and the gate slid open. A tall, dark figure rushed through the gate and tripped over the rope. With a yell of triumph, the guardsmen pounced on the monster.

The entire company came running when they heard the commotion, and the monster was pulled to its feet and marched inside. The governor's daughter, a very pretty girl of eighteen years, followed in the wake of the company, wringing her hands and sobbing softly. When deprived of its dark cloak and hat, the monster proved to be a handsome lad in his twen-ties. The stranger was from Pavonia. He admitted to leaping the wall around the time the windmill sails started moving on the new wind (which had given poor Jan Sol the impression that he had wings), but he would not say why he had come to New Amsterdam in such a nefarious fashion at such a late hour. This was a crime that was punishable by death. The governor was infuriated by the stubborn stranger who had invaded his home and sentenced him to death by hanging at sundown two days hence.

The governor's daughter turned pale when she heard the sentence. The next morning she came to her father, weeping bitterly, and begged for the life of the stranger, who was her husband. They had met on an excursion across the river, where he had rescued her from the attentions of a couple of drunkards who had accosted her. The governor was shocked by this disclosure. He was berating his sobbing daughter for her disobedience when Cornelius Van Vorst, the leader of the rival colony of Pavonia, was shown into his office. He had come to plead for the pardon of the young man, who was his son.

The governor of New Amsterdam disliked all Pavonians and his fury was further kindled by the disobedience of his daughter, who had married his rival's son. Sensing that a compromise was in order, Van Vorst suggested that he might be willing to give up his right to some prime riverfront property and to the shad fisheries if the governor of New Amsterdam would spare his son. Seeing her father waiver in his resolve to hang the young man, the daughter threw herself at his feet and pleaded once more for the life of her husband. Finally, the governor gave in. Young Van Vorst was pardoned, and the governor even gave his daughter and new son-in-law a house on Broad Street as a wedding gift.

Jan Sol continued to guard the gate on Wall Street, but the governor forbade him schnapps while he was on duty. Each time Jan Sol saw the governor's daughter and her new husband, he eyed them suspiciously. He was never convinced that the Pavonian man was the "monster" he had shot at on his watch. How could he be? It was obvious that the man had neither long teeth, nor wings, nor glowing eyes.

Jan Sol spent many a night by the gate on Wall Street waiting for the return of the monster, hoping to vindicate his story, but the monster never came.

Resources

Adams, Charles J. III. *New York City Ghost Stories.* Reading, Pa.: Exeter House Books, 1996.

Adams, William Howard. *Gouverneur Morris: An Independent Life.* New Haven, Conn.: Yale University Press, 2003.

The American Revolution (2001). *The Battle of White Plains.* theamericanrevolution.org/battles/bat_wpla.asp (accessed August 27, 2004).

Arduinna (2000). *La Chasse Gallerie.* www.ygora.net/nav/page_index/contes/contes/obscur/obscur_27.htm (accessed August 24, 2004).

Benincasa, Janis, ed. *I Walked the Road Again.* New York: Purple Mountain Press, 1994.

Berketa, Rick (2004). *Niagara Falls: The Maid of the Mist, a History.* www.niagarafrontier.com/maidmist.html (accessed August 1, 2004).

Botkin, B. A., ed. *New York City Folklore.* New York: Random House, Inc., 1956.

Bowen, DuWayne Leslie. *One More Story.* New York: Greenfield Review Press, 1991.

Brookhiser, Richard (2002). *The Forgotten Founding Father.* www.cityjournal.org/html/12_2_urbanities-the_forgotten .html (accessed August 14, 2004).

Chadwick, Ian (2001). *Biography of Henry Hudson.* www.ian chadwick.com/hudson (accessed July 22, 2004).

Charles, Veronika Martenova. *Maiden of the Mist.* New York: Stoddard Publishing Company Limited, 2001.

Cohen, Daniel. *Ghostly Tales of Love and Revenge.* New York: Putnam Publishing Group, 1992.

Cornplanter, J. J. *Legends of the Longhouse.* Philadelphia: J. B. Lippincott, 1938.

Encyclopedia of North American Indians *Montauk.* college.hmco.com/history/readerscomp/naind/html/na_ 023400_montauk.htm (accessed July 20, 2004).

From Revolution to Reconstruction (2003). *A Biography of Gouverneur Morris 1752–1816.* odur.let.rug.nl/~usa/B/ morris/morris.htm (accessed August 14, 2004).

Haunted Sites of New York. mywebpages.comcast.net/para investigator/NY/NewYork.html (accessed May 12, 2004).

Hos-McGrane, M. (1999). *Sinterklaas in the Netherlands.* www.internet-at-work.com/hos_mcgrane/holidays/abhishek .html (accessed August 3, 2004).

Husted, Shirley Cox. *Valley of the Ghosts.* New York: County of Monroe, 1982.

Jagendorf, M. A. *The Ghost of Peg-Leg Peter and Other Stories of Old New York.* New York: Vanguard Press, Inc, 1965.

Jones, Louis C. *Things That Go Bump in the Night.* New York: Hill and Wang, 1959.

Johnson, Mary Ann. *The Ghosts of Port Bryon.* New York: North Country Books, Inc., 1987.

Klees, Emerson. *Legends and Stories of the Finger Lakes Region.* New York: Friends of the Finger Lakes Publishing, 1995.

———. *More Legends and Stories of the Finger Lakes Region.* New York: Friends of the Finger Lakes Publishing, 1997.

LeBeau, Julie. *La Chasse-Galerie.* elfwood.lysator.liu.se/art/j/u/juliel/chasse.jpg.html (accessed August 24, 2004).

Le Blanc, Charles. *Contes et Légendes du Quebec.* Paris: Nathan, 1999.

Macken, Lynda Lee. *Adirondack Ghosts.* Forked River, N.J.: Black Cat Press, 2000.

———. *Adirondack Ghosts II.* Forked River, N.J.: Black Cat Press, 2003.

———. *Empire Ghosts.* Forked River, N.J.: Black Cat Press, 2004.

———. *Ghostly Gotham*. Forked River, N.J.: Black Cat Press, 2002.

Noel, Lynn (1989). *La Chasse-Galerie*. homepage.mac.com/ lynnoel/pubs/Chasse-Galerie.pdf (accessed August 24, 2004).

Pitkin, David J. *Saratoga County Ghosts*. New York: Aurora Publications, 1998.

Saint Nicholas Center (2002). *Who is Saint Nicholas?* www.stnicholascenter.org/Brix?pageID=38 (accessed July 7, 2004).

Sceurman, Mark, and Mark Moran, eds. *Captain Kidd on the Raritan Bay, Weird NJ*. Vol. 14. www.njhm.com/captain kiddstory.htm (accessed September 4, 2004).

Shepherd, Aaron (1995). *The Baker's Dozen*. www.aaron shep.com/rt/RTE09.html (accessed July 18, 2004).

Shultis, Neva. *From Sunset to Cock's Crow*. New York: Three Geese in Flight Books, 1957.

Skinner, Charles M. *American Myths and Legends*, Vol. I. Philadelphia: J. B. Lippincott Company, 1903.

———. *Myths and Legends of Our Own Land*, Vol. II. Philadelphia: J. B. Lippincott Company, 1896.

The Straight Dope Science Advisory Board (2002). *What's the Origin of "Baker's Dozen"?* www.straightdope.com/mailbag/ mbakersdozen.html (accessed July 18, 2004).

Strange Happenings Ghost and Hauntings Research Society (2003). *Haunted Places, Ghosts, and Hauntings in New York.* www.strangehappenings.methyus.com/New-York-Hauntings.htm (accessed August 16, 2004).

Thompson, Harold W. *New York State Folktales, Legends, and Ballads.* New York: Dover Publications, Inc., 1939.

Tice, Joyce M. (2000). *Internet Listing of Hessian Soldiers of the Revolution.* members.tripod.com/~Silvie/Hessian.html (accessed August 27, 2004).

Tolnay, Tom, *Spirits of the Adirondack Mountains.* New York: Birch Brook Press, 2001.

Ward, Mason, ed. *I Always Tell the Truth (Even If I Have to Lie to Do It!).* New York: Greenfield Review Press, 1990.

Winfield, Mason. *Shadows of the Western Door.* Buffalo, N.Y.: Western New York Wares, Inc., 1997.

———. *Spirits of the Great Hill.* Buffalo, N.Y.: Western New York Wares, Inc., 2001.

About the Author

S. E. Schlosser has been telling stories since she was a child, when games of "let's pretend" quickly built themselves into full-length stories acted out with friends. A graduate of the Institute of Children's Literature and Rutgers University, she created and maintains the Web site AmericanFolklore.net, where she shares a wealth of stories from all fifty states, some dating back to the origins of America. Sandy spends much of her time answering questions from visitors to the site. Many of her favorite e-mails come from other folklorists who delight in practicing the old tradition of who can tell the tallest tale.